MARQUIS
de LAFAYETTE

MARQUIS de LAFAYETTE

Pierre Horn

CHELSEA HOUSE PUBLISHERS
NEW YORK
PHILADELPHIA

Chelsea House Publishers
EDITOR-IN-CHIEF: Nancy Toff
EXECUTIVE EDITOR: Remmel T. Nunn
MANAGING EDITOR: Karyn Gullen Browne
COPY CHIEF: Juliann Barbato
PICTURE EDITOR: Adrian G. Allen
ART DIRECTOR: Giannella Garrett
MANUFACTURING EDITOR: Gerald Levine

World Leaders — Past & Present
SENIOR EDITOR: John W. Selfridge

Staff for MARQUIS de LAFAYETTE:
COPY EDITOR: Karen Hammonds
DEPUTY COPY CHIEF: Ellen Scordato
EDITORIAL ASSISTANT: Sean Ginty
PICTURE RESEARCHER: Lisa Kirchner
DESIGNER: David Murray
PRODUCTION COORDINATOR: Joseph Romano
COVER ILLUSTRATION: Dominick Finelle

First Printing

1 3 5 7 9 8 6 4 2

Library of Congress Cataloging in Publication Data

Horn, Pierre L.
    Marquis de Lafayette.

    (World leaders past & present)
    Bibliography: p.
    Includes index.
    Summary: Traces the life of the French general and statesman who was
instrumental in persuading France to aid the colonists in the American Revolution
and then returned to participate in the political scene in his own country.
    1. Lafayette, Marie Joseph Paul Yves Roch Gilbert
Du Motier, marquis de, 1757–1834—Juvenile
literature. 2. France—History—1789–1815—Juvenile
literature. 3. Generals—France—Biography—Juvenile
literture. 4. France. Armée—Biography—Juvenile
literature. 5. Generals—United States—Biography—
Juvenile literature. 6. United States. Army—
Biography—Juvenile literature. 7. Statesmen—
France—Biography—Juvenile literature. 8. United
States—History—Revolution, 1775–1783—
Participation, French—Juvenile literature.
[1. Lafayette, Marie Joseph Paul Yves Roch Gilbert Du
Motier, marquis de, 1757–1834. 2. Generals.
3. Statesmen] I. Title. II. Series.
DC146.L2H67   1988   944.04'092'4 [B]
[92]   87-32645

ISBN 1-55546-813-6

Contents

John Adams
John Quincy Adams
Konrad Adenauer
Alexander the Great
Salvador Allende
Marc Antony
Corazon Aquino
Yasir Arafat
King Arthur
Hafez al-Assad
Kemal Atatürk
Attila
Clement Attlee
Augustus Caesar
Menachem Begin
David Ben-Gurion
Otto von Bismarck
Léon Blum
Simon Bolívar
Cesare Borgia
Willy Brandt
Leonid Brezhnev
Julius Caesar
John Calvin
Jimmy Carter
Fidel Castro
Catherine the Great
Charlemagne
Chiang Kai-Shek
Winston Churchill
Georges Clemenceau
Cleopatra
Constantine the Great
Hernán Cortés
Oliver Cromwell
Georges-Jacques
    Danton
Jefferson Davis
Moshe Dayan
Charles de Gaulle
Eamon De Valera
Eugene Debs
Deng Xiaoping
Benjamin Disraeli
Alexander Dubček
François & Jean-Claude
    Duvalier
Dwight Eisenhower
Eleanor of Aquitaine
Elizabeth i
Faisal
Ferdinand & Isabella
Francisco Franco
Benjamin Franklin

Frederick the Great
Indira Gandhi
Mohandas Gandhi
Giuseppe Garibaldi
Amin & Bashir Gemayel
Genghis Khan
William Gladstone
Mikhail Gorbachev
Ulysses S. Grant
Ernesto "Che" Guevara
Tenzin Gyatso
Alexander Hamilton
Dag Hammarskjöld
Henry viii
Henry of Navarre
Paul von Hindenburg
Hirohito
Adolf Hitler
Ho Chi Minh
King Hussein
Ivan the Terrible
Andrew Jackson
James i
Wojciech Jaruzelski
Thomas Jefferson
Joan of Arc
Pope John xxiii
Pope John Paul ii
Lyndon Johnson
Benito Juárez
John Kennedy
Robert Kennedy
Jomo Kenyatta
Ayatollah Khomeini
Nikita Khrushchev
Kim Il Sung
Martin Luther King, Jr.
Henry Kissinger
Kublai Khan
Lafayette
Robert E. Lee
Vladimir Lenin
Abraham Lincoln
David Lloyd George
Louis xiv
Martin Luther
Judas Maccabeus
James Madison
Nelson & Winnie
    Mandela
Mao Zedong
Ferdinand Marcos
George Marshall

Mary, Queen of Scots
Tomáš Masaryk
Golda Meir
Klemens von Metternich
James Monroe
Hosni Mubarak
Robert Mugabe
Benito Mussolini
Napoléon Bonaparte
Gamal Abdel Nasser
Jawaharlal Nehru
Nero
Nicholas II
Richard Nixon
Kwame Nkrumah
Daniel Ortega
Mohammed Reza Pahlavi
Thomas Paine
Charles Stewart
    Parnell
Pericles
Juan Perón
Peter the Great
Pol Pot
Muammar el-Qaddafi
Ronald Reagan
Cardinal Richelieu
Maximilien Robespierre
Eleanor Roosevelt
Franklin Roosevelt
Theodore Roosevelt
Anwar Sadat
Haile Selassie
Prince Sihanouk
Jan Smuts
Joseph Stalin
Sukarno
Sun Yat-sen
Tamerlane
Mother Teresa
Margaret Thatcher
Josip Broz Tito
Toussaint L'Ouverture
Leon Trotsky
Pierre Trudeau
Harry Truman
Queen Victoria
Lech Walesa
George Washington
Chaim Weizmann
Woodrow Wilson
Xerxes
Emiliano Zapata
Zhou Enlai

CHELSEA HOUSE PUBLISHERS

ON LEADERSHIP

Arthur M. Schlesinger, jr.

Leadership, it may be said, is really what makes the world go round. Love no doubt smooths the passage; but love is a private transaction between consenting adults. Leadership is a public transaction with history. The idea of leadership affirms the capacity of individuals to move, inspire, and mobilize masses of people so that they act together in pursuit of an end. Sometimes leadership serves good purposes, sometimes bad; but whether the end is benign or evil, great leaders are those men and women who leave their personal stamp on history.

Now, the very concept of leadership implies the proposition that individuals can make a difference. This proposition has never been universally accepted. From classical times to the present day, eminent thinkers have regarded individuals as no more than the agents and pawns of larger forces, whether the gods and goddesses of the ancient world or, in the modern era, race, class, nation, the dialectic, the will of the people, the spirit of the times, history itself. Against such forces, the individual dwindles into insignificance.

So contends the thesis of historical determinism. Tolstoy's great novel *War and Peace* offers a famous statement of the case. Why, Tolstoy asked, did millions of men in the Napoleonic Wars, denying their human feelings and their common sense, move back and forth across Europe slaughtering their fellows? "The war," Tolstoy answered, "was bound to happen simply because it was bound to happen." All prior history predetermined it. As for leaders, they, Tolstoy said, "are but the labels that serve to give a name to an end and, like labels, they have the least possible connection with the event." The greater the leader, "the more conspicuous the inevitability and the predestination of every act he commits." The leader, said Tolstoy, is "the slave of history."

Determinism takes many forms. Marxism is the determinism of class. Nazism the determinism of race. But the idea of men and women as the slaves of history runs athwart the deepest human instincts. Rigid determinism abolishes the idea of human freedom—

the assumption of free choice that underlies every move we make, every word we speak, every thought we think. It abolishes the idea of human responsibility, since it is manifestly unfair to reward or punish people for actions that are by definition beyond their control. No one can live consistently by any deterministic creed. The Marxist states prove this themselves by their extreme susceptibility to the cult of leadership.

More than that, history refutes the idea that individuals make no difference. In December 1931 a British politician crossing Park Avenue in New York City between 76th and 77th Streets around 10:30 P.M. looked in the wrong direction and was knocked down by an automobile—a moment, he later recalled, of a man aghast, a world aglare: "I do not understand why I was not broken like an eggshell or squashed like a gooseberry." Fourteen months later an American politician, sitting in an open car in Miami, Florida, was fired on by an assassin; the man beside him was hit. Those who believe that individuals make no difference to history might well ponder whether the next two decades would have been the same had Mario Constasino's car killed Winston Churchill in 1931 and Giuseppe Zangara's bullet killed Franklin Roosevelt in 1933. Suppose, in addition, that Adolf Hitler had been killed in the street fighting during the Munich *Putsch* of 1923 and that Lenin had died of typhus during World War I. What would the 20th century be like now?

For better or for worse, individuals do make a difference. "The notion that a people can run itself and its affairs anonymously," wrote the philosopher William James, "is now well known to be the silliest of absurdities. Mankind does nothing save through initiatives on the part of inventors, great or small, and imitation by the rest of us—these are the sole factors in human progress. Individuals of genius show the way, and set the patterns, which common people then adopt and follow."

Leadership, James suggests, means leadership in thought as well as in action. In the long run, leaders in thought may well make the greater difference to the world. But, as Woodrow Wilson once said, "Those only are leaders of men, in the general eye, who lead in action. . . . It is at their hands that new thought gets its translation into the crude language of deeds." Leaders in thought often invent in solitude and obscurity, leaving to later generations the tasks of imitation. Leaders in action—the leaders portrayed in this series—have to be effective in their own time.

And they cannot be effective by themselves. They must act in response to the rhythms of their age. Their genius must be adapted, in a phrase of William James's, "to the receptivities of the moment." Leaders are useless without followers. "There goes the mob," said the French politician hearing a clamor in the streets. "I am their leader. I must follow them." Great leaders turn the inchoate emotions of the mob to purposes of their own. They seize on the opportunities of their time, the hopes, fears, frustrations, crises, potentialities. They succeed when events have prepared the way for them, when the community is awaiting to be aroused, when they can provide the clarifying and organizing ideas. Leadership ignites the circuit between the individual and the mass and thereby alters history.

It may alter history for better or for worse. Leaders have been responsible for the most extravagant follies and most monstrous crimes that have beset suffering humanity. They have also been vital in such gains as humanity has made in individual freedom, religious and racial tolerance, social justice, and respect for human rights.

There is no sure way to tell in advance who is going to lead for good and who for evil. But a glance at the gallery of men and women in *World Leaders—Past and Present* suggests some useful tests.

One test is this: Do leaders lead by force or by persuasion? By command or by consent? Through most of history leadership was exercised by the divine right of authority. The duty of followers was to defer and to obey. "Theirs not to reason why / Theirs but to do and die." On occasion, as with the so-called enlightened despots of the 18th century in Europe, absolutist leadership was animated by humane purposes. More often, absolutism nourished the passion for domination, land, gold, and conquest and resulted in tyranny.

The great revolution of modern times has been the revolution of equality. The idea that all people should be equal in their legal condition has undermined the old structure of authority, hierarchy, and deference. The revolution of equality has had two contrary effects on the nature of leadership. For equality, as Alexis de Tocqueville pointed out in his great study *Democracy in America*, might mean equality in servitude as well as equality in freedom.

"I know of only two methods of establishing equality in the political world," Tocqueville wrote. "Rights must be given to every citizen, or none at all to anyone . . . save one, who is the master of all." There was no middle ground "between the sovereignty of all and the absolute power of one man." In his astonishing prediction of 20th-century totalitarian dictatorship, Tocqueville explained how the revolution of equality could lead to the *"Führerprinzip"* and more terrible absolutism than the world had ever known.

But when rights are given to every citizen and the sovereignty of all is established, the problem of leadership takes a new form, becomes more exacting than ever before. It is easy to issue commands and enforce them by the rope and the stake, the concentration camp and the *gulag.* It is much harder to use argument and achievement to overcome opposition and win consent. The Founding Fathers of the United States understood the difficulty. They believed that history had given them the opportunity to decide, as Alexander Hamilton wrote in the first Federalist Paper, whether men are indeed capable of basing government on "reflection and choice, or whether they are forever destined to depend . . . on accident and force."

Government by reflection and choice called for a new style of leadership and a new quality of followership. It required leaders to be responsive to popular concerns, and it required followers to be active and informed participants in the process. Democracy does not eliminate emotion from politics; sometimes it fosters demagoguery; but it is confident that, as the greatest of democratic leaders put it, you cannot fool all of the people all of the time. It measures leadership by results and retires those who overreach or falter or fail.

It is true that in the long run despots are measured by results too. But they can postpone the day of judgment, sometimes indefinitely, and in the meantime they can do infinite harm. It is also true that democracy is no guarantee of virtue and intelligence in government, for the voice of the people is not necessarily the voice of God. But democracy, by assuring the right of opposition, offers built-in resistance to the evils inherent in absolutism. As the theologian Reinhold Niebuhr summed it up, "Man's capacity for justice makes democracy possible, but man's inclination to injustice makes democracy necessary."

A second test for leadership is the end for which power is sought. When leaders have as their goal the supremacy of a master race or the promotion of totalitarian revolution or the acquisition and exploitation of colonies or the protection of greed and privilege or the preservation of personal power, it is likely that their leadership will do little to advance the cause of humanity. When their goal is the abolition of slavery, the liberation of women, the enlargement of opportunity for the poor and powerless, the extension of equal rights to racial minorities, the defense of the freedoms of expression and opposition, it is likely that their leadership will increase the sum of human liberty and welfare.

Leaders have done great harm to the world. They have also conferred great benefits. You will find both sorts in this series. Even "good" leaders must be regarded with a certain wariness. Leaders are not demigods; they put on their trousers one leg after another just like ordinary mortals. No leader is infallible, and every leader needs to be reminded of this at regular intervals. Irreverence irritates leaders but is their salvation. Unquestioning submission corrupts leaders and demeans followers. Making a cult of a leader is always a mistake. Fortunately hero worship generates its own antidote. "Every hero," said Emerson, "becomes a bore at last."

The signal benefit the great leaders confer is to embolden the rest of us to live according to our own best selves, to be active, insistent, and resolute in affirming our own sense of things. For great leaders attest to the reality of human freedom against the supposed inevitabilities of history. And they attest to the wisdom and power that may lie within the most unlikely of us, which is why Abraham Lincoln remains the supreme example of great leadership. A great leader, said Emerson, exhibits new possibilities to all humanity. "We feed on genius. . . . Great men exist that there may be greater men."

Great leaders, in short, justify themselves by emancipating and empowering their followers. So humanity struggles to master its destiny, remembering with Alexis de Tocqueville: "It is true that around every man a fatal circle is traced beyond which he cannot pass; but within the wide verge of that circle he is powerful and free; as it is with man, so with communities."

1

Young Dreams of Glory

Fourteen-year-old Gilbert de Lafayette sat at his desk and looked at the assignment his teacher had just written on the board: "Write an essay on the perfect horse." Gilbert thought for several minutes and, then, as though inspired, began to write feverishly. He knew that his classmates would paint an idealized portrait that would emphasize the horse's physical characteristics — its proportions, its gait, its discipline, perhaps its temperament.

Gilbert, however, chose to praise the animal's dignity, giving as an example the horse that, upon seeing the raised whip, unseats its rider. He concluded his composition by stating that liberty is always preferable to complacent obedience. In time, Lafayette would become convinced that all people yearned to be free and would in the end rise up against their oppressors regardless of the consequences.

> *It appears that he was more ambitious of what he regarded as true, than of the honors of the college.*
> —WILLIAM CUTTER
> historian

Marie Joseph Paul Yves Roch Gilbert du Motier de Lafayette was born into an aristocratic family on September 6, 1757, at the Chateau de Chavaniac in Auvergne, France. As a boy, Lafayette was cared for by his grandmother and aunts.

This 1779 cartoon portrays the American colonies as an untamed horse throwing off the reins of its British master. It refers to the War of Independence, in which the colonies rebelled against England.

Later in life, this highly privileged member of a privileged social class would respond with enthusiasm and optimism both to the news of the American Declaration of Independence and, above all, to the French Revolution, with its call for "liberty, equality, fraternity." He even declared in a February 20, 1790, speech, a year after the turmoil began, "The old order was but servitude; and in this case insurrection is the most sacred of duties." His schoolboy respect for righteous rebellion, acts of courage and nobility, had evolved into a vigorous defense of freedom lovers and disinherited masses everywhere.

Marie Joseph Paul Yves Roch Gilbert du Motier de La Fayette was born on September 6, 1757, at the château of Chavaniac, a castle in the central French province of Auvergne. Gilbert never knew his father, Colonel Michel de La Fayette, who was away fighting in the Seven Years' War against the British and German armies when his son was born and died in battle two years later at the age of 27.

Although the La Fayettes were an old aristocratic family, they lived modestly, for their lands produced little and their court connections were almost non-existent. Thus, as soon as was decently practical, Madame (Mme.) de La Fayette moved to Paris to live with her parents, the La Rivières, the better to work on behalf of little Gilbert. Gilbert was left in the care of his paternal grandmother, Mme. du Motier, a formidable woman who ruled her household with vigor and compassion, and two aunts. Mme. du Motier applied to and received from King Louis XV an annual pension of 600 *livres* (about $3,000) to help educate the colonel's son. At first, Gilbert learned the basics from the village priest, who also taught him the then-radical notion that wealth and merit were not synonymous and that moral courage often was better than physical bravery. Later, he was entrusted to another cleric, Abbé Fayon. With him he studied French history and literature, mathematics, Latin, and whatever English the abbot knew. A cousin wrote in his memoirs that on visiting the Lafayettes in 1768, he found the 11-year-old Gilbert "singularly learned for his age, astonishingly advanced in his thought and his reasoning, and extraordinary by his reflections, his maturity, his moderation, coolness and judgement."

This baroque painting depicts Louis XV lunching with members of the French court and army. Louis was king of France from 1715 to 1774, and his ineffectual rule contributed to the decline of royal authority and the outbreak of revolution in 1789.

The young marquis stands beside his mother, Julie de la Rivière, holding a portrait of his cousin, Mlle. de Chavaniac. Lafayette was separated from his mother as a child and upon her death was orphaned at age 13.

In the severe atmosphere of the castle, a massive building with two round towers, lost in one of the poorest provinces of France yet with a fine view of the Massif Central mountains, the young boy enjoyed a childhood filled with stories of great military feats. Again and again he heard about the exploits of his dead father, whose memory was revered at Chavaniac, and of his illustrious ancestors. Gilbert longed to show his strength and fearlessness, too. When he heard that a wild animal known as the "Beast of Gevaudan" was killing sheep and pigs and generally terrorizing the local inhabitants, he set out at the age of eight to kill it with his sword. He believed that as lord of the region, his duty was to protect his people and their possessions. Unfortunately for Gilbert's dreams of glory, the "Beast" was actually a very large wolf and was shot down by a royal hunter and sent as a gift to the king. Many other opportunities to prove his valor and courage would come his way, however. In 1768, at 11, Gilbert was sent to Paris to rejoin his mother. She enrolled him at one of the best private schools in the city, the Collège du Plessis, not only to finish his formal education but also to learn the ways of the court and courtiers and to train in the Black Musketeers. He would spend four years preparing for his court appearance and his commission. By his own account, he was an excellent student, though perhaps too questioning of authority. In 1770, the young man experienced two losses: His mother died after a brief illness, and a few weeks later her father died as well. Still, Gilbert did not seem to be overly distraught. He had few contacts with his mother and hardly any with his grandfather; moreover, stoicism — indifference (or apparent indifference) to pleasure and pain — had been drilled into him ever since he was a child. Furthermore, he was well aware of his position and what was expected of him. The 13-year-old Marquis de La Fayette was now a very rich young man.

Lafayette's father-in-law, the Duke d'Ayen-Noailles, headed one of the most powerful families in France. D'Ayen strongly opposed Lafayette's mission to aid the American colonies.

Lafayette married Adrienne D'Ayen-Noailles on April 11, 1774. A bride at 14, she bore Lafayette 3 children and was a devout supporter of her husband throughout his revolutionary campaigns.

Whereas his father's family was considered poor (and nobles were forbidden to work), his mother's was quite wealthy. Grandfather La Rivière had left Gilbert an income of 120,000 livres ($600,000) a year in addition to large estates in the French provinces of Touraine and Brittany. He now was a highly eligible bachelor, and marriage in one's early teens was customary.

Gilbert continued his schooling at the Collège du Plessis and also attended a prestigious military school, the Académie de Versailles. There he learned the fine points of command, marching and riding, shooting, and fencing, at which he excelled. Among his blue-blood classmates was the Count of Artois, the king's grandson — a young man he instantly disliked.

Meanwhile, according to custom, his great-grandfather and legal guardian, the Count de la Rivière, was making arrangements for Gilbert's marriage. Thanks to their noble name and vast fortune, the count set his sights very high. He entered into negotiations with the Ayen-Noailles, one of the four wealthiest families in France, having asked on Gilbert's behalf for the hand of their second daughter, 12-year-old Adrienne. Despite the settlement arrived at by Monsieur (M.) de la Rivière and the Duke d'Ayen, Mme. d'Ayen demanded that she judge the prospective bridegroom's quality for herself, that the wedding be postponed for two years, and that the adolescent couple live in a wing of the Noailles mansion in Paris. When Lafayette was told of the impending match and of the approval of the girl's mother, he was more than pleased, and Adrienne was ecstatic: Both had fallen in love with one another.

The wedding took place on April 11, 1774, attended by the king and his grandchildren (the future Louis XVI and Charles X). As a dowry, Adrienne brought Gilbert 200,000 livres and social and political connections beyond compare; all who knew the ambitious Ayens expected them to work hard on behalf of their new son-in-law. Gilbert was 16; his bride, 14.

Costume balls rose to the height of popularity in the courts of Louis XIV and Louis XV. Louis XIV promoted these lavish affairs as a way of distracting the nobility from political concerns.

The two teenagers were an interesting couple. Red-headed and freckle-faced, Gilbert was thin, awkward, unsophisticated, reserved to the point of shyness, and occasionally even dull. But he also was kind and generous, enthusiastic, tender and loving, and in small groups quite charming. He could, in fact, be rather entertaining and droll, sometimes even acid tongued, as when he quashed the future Louis XVIII. The royal prince was proud of his fantastic memory and made no secret of the fact; finally Lafayette, paraphrasing Shakespeare, responded, "Everybody knows that memory is the wit of fools!"

Adrienne was a tall and very pretty girl, with blond hair and blue eyes. Like her four sisters, she had received a good education from her mother, reading aloud the famous works of the French classical theater. All the girls had been allowed to think for themselves and to value courage and virtue above all else. Moreover, Adrienne was an intelligent and sensible adviser, fiercely loyal and devoted, an excellent money manager, a tolerant and affectionate wife and helpmate.

Louis XVI was the last of the Bourbon kings to rule France. A lazy and inept monarch, he sided with the nobility and the Catholic clergy during the French Revolution and refused to accept the idea of a constitutional monarchy.

Queen Marie Antoinette reigned with King Louis XVI. Her extravagant expenditures contributed to France's massive debt during the 1780s and provoked growing unrest among the starving peasantry.

Two months after the wedding, however, King Louis XV — to almost no one's regret — died of smallpox, and his oldest grandson was crowned Louis XVI, with Marie Antoinette as his queen. Thanks to the Ayens' influence, Lafayette soon received a captain's commission in the Noailles Dragoons, in which his immediate superior was Adrienne's cousin and the commanding general's adjutant was his brother-in-law, the Viscount de Noailles.

In September 1774, Lafayette had to join his regiment in Metz, one of the more pleasant French garrison towns (military posts), in the Lorraine region of eastern France. By day he attended army maneuvers, drilled soldiers and horses, and perfected his marching style. In the evening, he enjoyed the company of ladies, who found him quite charming. Many who knew him then wrote about the young officer's popularity both with his men and with the local gentry. For his part, Lafayette wrote to his new bride of his undying love — adding that his calendar was quite busy with social calls and evening entertainments. Adrienne probably was aware of her husband's appeal to women, but ever tolerant where he was concerned, she was willing to overlook his conduct.

A member of the French National Guard woos a barmaid during the 1800s. The first unit of the National Guard was formed in Paris by Lafayette after the fall of the Bastille. He later became its commandant-general.

On his return to the capital a few months later, Lafayette resumed his existence at court and in Paris, where, according to one account, "he received many people and served very good dinners." In addition, less from genuine interest than from a wish to be accepted, he belonged to the most elegant, trendy group surrounding the empty-headed, decadent Queen Marie Antoinette — even though she had made fun of him when he fell during a palace ball. Lafayette would never forget the insult, however, nor would the queen forget his oafishness.

This company of wild friends, which included the Viscount de Noailles and other members of the high nobility, was called "the Society of the Wooden Sword," in honor of the tavern where their revelries usually took place. Lafayette often had difficulty keeping up with the crowd — especially with his sophisticated brother-in-law, whose admiration he badly wanted. Once, in the middle of a "successful" binge, for example, he kept reminding his friends to be sure to tell his brother-in-law that he had drunk a great deal. What is more, because an aristocrat had to have a mistress to be fully accepted by his peers, Gilbert decided to pursue one of the court beauties, Countess Aglaé d'Hunolstein. Unknown to the would-be seducer, however, was that Aglaé was already the mistress of the Duke de Chartres, a far grander lover, because he was a royal prince and first cousin to the king. The countess rejected Lafayette, whereupon he promptly assumed that she was in love with the Count de Ségur and challenged the innocent man to a duel. After much time and diplomacy, Lafayette's friends calmed the hothead down. He then was packed off again to Metz, in order to avoid further ridicule and embarrassment. Adrienne was pregnant.

In August 1775, several months after fighting between the British and the American revolutionaries began at Lexington and Concord, Massachusetts, Lafayette and his brother-in-law attended a gathering that made a tremendous impression on the 18-year-old soldier. The occasion was a dinner given by the Duke de Broglie, commander in chief of the Metz garrison and marshal of France, in honor of the Duke of Gloucester, a brother of King George III of England. Not only did Lafayette hear the British prince speak of the American colonists' right to full representation in Parliament, but he also heard that an army was being raised by one General George Washington. Earlier he had read with great interest a political treatise by Abbé Raynal in which two sentences particularly impressed him: "Liberty is the citizens' enjoyment of their rights" and "The sovereignty of a people resides in the accomplishment of its will."

Because those ideas had meant so much to Lafayette when he first read them, it was natural that he listened to Gloucester so enthusiastically. "My heart had been enrolled," he wrote later.

George Washington commanded the American army, to which Lafayette was appointed major-general. The first U.S. president was like a father to Lafayette and greatly influenced his strong advocacy of liberty.

In the fall, Gilbert returned to Paris. There he followed developments in the American situation; watched over his wife, who gave birth to a baby girl in December; and was initiated into the Freemasons, a fraternal organization whose tenets included social justice, popular will, and scientific progress as the bases for individual happiness. In June 1776, the reform- and economy-minded war minister placed many junior officers, including Lafayette, on the reserve list, thereby freeing the young captain of all legal restraints that came with military status. At this time the Duke de Broglie introduced a protégé of his, Johann de Kalb, and Lafayette to the American delegate to France, Silas Deane.

Deane's mission was to obtain French help — financial, military, diplomatic — for the revolutionary cause, and he thought that he could more easily sway King Louis XVI's government if he enlisted members of the French aristocracy in the American

The American delegate to France, Silas Deane (right), meets with Lafayette (left) and Baron Johann de Kalb (center), a brigadier general in the French army. The two liberal aristocrats were secretly enlisted by Deane to fight for the American colonies.

army. Impressed by the influential connections described by de Broglie, Deane gave the 19-year-old Lafayette the unheard-of rank of major general — but at no pay, as specified in the contract. De Kalb, too, signed on as a major general, but at least he had been in war and had field experience.

Lafayette knew that the French king would want to prevent his and de Kalb's departure for the new nation so that France would not seem to be allied with the Americans. Furthermore, his father-in-law would absolutely disapprove of such a reckless undertaking. Thus, Lafayette secretly purchased a cargo ship, aptly named *La Victoire*, to sail out of Bordeaux. When his father-in-law, the Duke d'Ayen, and the king learned of his plans, they immediately issued orders forbidding his departure and threatened imprisonment for all involved. Instead of being the obedient son and subject, Lafayette cleverly had his ship moved to Los Pasajes, a suburb of San Sebastian, in northern Spain. He sailed on April 20, 1777.

The crossing was long, taking more than seven weeks, and very uncomfortable. Most of the volunteers, including Lafayette, became seasick. Life on board was rather boring, but Lafayette used his confinement to improve his English and especially to write long letters to Adrienne, whom he had left without a good-bye and who was again pregnant.

Some of Lafayette's letters to Adrienne are quite revealing, not only of his affection for her but also of his conception of the United States as ideal and symbol. In a letter dated June 7, 1777, he writes, "The happiness of America is intimately linked to the happiness of all humanity; she will become the respectable and sure haven for virtue, honesty, tolerance, equality, peaceful liberty."

At last, on June 13, *La Victoire* anchored off Georgetown, South Carolina. After making their way through swamps for several hours, Lafayette, de Kalb, and a small party arrived at the plantation house of a patriot, Major Benjamin Huger, who greeted them with a warm welcome.

The great American adventure had begun.

Lafayette prepares to board his ship, *La Victoire*, to sail to the American colonies. The ship secretly departed from Los Pasajes in northern Spain in order to escape detection by the French king, who at first opposed France's involvement in the American revolution.

2

The Road to Yorktown

After spending what seemed an endless time at sea, the French volunteers were delighted at being greeted by such a gentleman as Major Benjamin Huger. And when the aristocrats' intention to join Washington's army became known around Charleston, they were feted everywhere by the local notables. This series of receptions, which included strange foods such as barbecued meats, made a lasting impression on the young Lafayette, who later recalled with pleasure the short time he spent in South Carolina.

On June 22, 1777, the French party took its leave of southern hospitality and set out for Philadelphia, home of the Continental Congress. If the crossing had been hard, the month-long journey through the backwoods seemed even worse. Because few roads existed, Lafayette and his companions had to ride or walk through swamps and dense forests, often abandoning equipment along the way. Frequently they were forced to camp out in the wilderness, for inns were extremely rare. The summer heat, the rain, the humidity, and the bugs made the journey even more difficult.

He is a prodigy for his age, full of courage, spirit, judgment, feelings of generosity and zeal for the cause of liberty on this continent.
—BRIGADIER GENERAL DE KALB
on Lafayette

Lafayette as a young major-general. The marquis proved himself a skillful soldier during his two-year service in the Continental Army and was appointed commander of a division in Virginia.

Never one to criticize America, Lafayette, who called the United States "the most wonderful country on earth," preferred to accentuate the positive. For all its difficulties, the 800-mile trek did allow him to explore the American wilderness.

At the end of July 1777, the party finally arrived in Philadelphia, tired and bedraggled, eager to present themselves to representatives of Congress and receive their military assignments. They were terribly shocked, therefore, to learn not only that they were not going to be commissioned into the army; they were also strongly advised to return to France as soon as possible. Had Lafayette incurred the wrath of his king and his father-in-law, endured

A depiction of the beginnings of an American settlement on the left and its completion as a farming estate on the right. Lafayette was deeply impressed by the untamed beauty of the American wilderness and later described America as "the most beautiful country on earth."

physical pain, bore all sorts of discomforts, and wasted his money all for nothing?

Shaken but surprisingly determined, the Marquis de Lafayette wrote a short note to James Lowell, chairman of the Committee on Foreign Applications: "After the sacrifices I have made for the cause of independence, I think I have the right to request two favors: first, to serve without salary and at my expense; secondly, to serve as a volunteer." He also made sure to enclose a letter of recommendation that he had received from Benjamin Franklin in which the respected statesman wrote of the young marquis's great wealth and important court connections.

Lafayette's direction brought results within a few days. On July 31, the Continental Congress passed a resolution to thank the generous young man and, most important, to appoint him to the rank of major general. The other Frenchmen, with the exception of de Kalb, were reimbursed for their expenses and dismissed.

The next evening, Gilbert de Lafayette attended a dinner party at which, for the first time, he met George Washington. Lafayette was impressed with the American commander in chief, and later commented on "the majesty of his face and his tallness, his noble and friendly way of greeting officers and citizens alike." In turn, Washington, who took Lafayette aside after the dinner and spoke with him for more than an hour, liked the attentive and admiring new major general. In Lafayette he discerned intelligence and courage as well as a definite talent for leadership. Their mutual affection would never diminish.

Lafayette is helped off his horse after being shot in the thigh during the Battle of Brandywine, near Philadelphia. The young commander had bravely directed troops from the front line and impressed many with his zeal and ardor.

General Washington monitors the Battle of Yorktown from the trenches in 1781.

In the summer of 1777, the Continental army was in a very poor and demoralized condition. General Horatio Gates had just lost the Battle of Ticonderoga, leaving Pennsylvania open to the British, who were ready to pounce from the north, while in the south English ships were approaching Chesapeake Bay, heading toward Philadelphia. Unfortunately, conflicting intelligence reports about the enemy's strategy raised so many doubts in Washington's mind that instead of holding a firm defensive position at Brandywine Creek as he had planned, he moved his troops from place to place until defeat was inevitable.

Lafayette was desperate to stop his militia's flight. He rode to the front line and proceeded to cajole and threaten his men. By that time, English sharpshooters had seen his dark blue, white, and gold general's uniform and begun to shoot at him. Unconcerned, he continued to direct maneuvers and was then shot in the thigh. In the heat of battle, however, he hardly noticed his wound, and it was not until blood started to run into his boot that he agreed to be taken to a doctor. His men, perhaps because they had not been accustomed to such ardor and bravery, stood firm long enough to retreat in an orderly fashion. Major General Marquis de Lafayette had just turned 20 years old.

Benjamin Franklin, the American printer, publisher, inventor, and scientist, served as the ambassador to France during the Revolution. The friendly scholar defended Lafayette, aiding his entry into the Continental Army and his subsequent reconciliation with the French court.

The Americans had suffered a grave defeat, for they had abandoned the field, along with weapons and artillery, and 1,300 men were dead, captured, or wounded. On September 26, the Continental Congress was forced to leave Philadelphia, because the British were about to invade the city, despite Washington's valiant efforts. In his report to the Board of War, the commander in chief ruefully wrote, "I hope another time we shall compensate for the losses now sustained." While Washington moved the bulk of his troops to Valley Forge, in southeastern Pennsylvania, in preparation for the winter, General Gates pursued the Hessian mercenaries (hired German soldiers) led by the British general John Burgoyne. He beat them first at Freeman's Farm and then captured the trapped enemy army at Saratoga on October 17, 1777.

In Paris and at Versailles, the sad news of the defeat at Brandywine and the fall of Philadelphia was softened somewhat by Gates's two great victories and, to a lesser extent, by Lafayette's fearless exploits. (From his post in France, Benjamin Franklin was informing Congress that many influential Frenchmen were now supporting the American cause, thanks in part to "their" major general.)

As soon as he could, Lafayette wrote his wife that his wound was "nothing, and the bullet touched neither bone nor nerve." Later, while convalescing in Bethlehem, Pennsylvania, the marquis advised Adrienne — "as the wife of an American general officer" — to defend the conduct of the war to any doubters. He also begged her for news from home. He still did not know that on July 1, 1777, Adrienne had given birth to another little girl, Anastasie.

After he returned to service, he constantly badgered Washington for a command of his own and finally received one after he again proved himself during a successful raid on a Hessian camp near Haddonfield, New Jersey. In that encounter, he showed resourcefulness and skill, vigor and intelligence. He was indeed becoming a very good field commander.

Washington first met Lafayette at a dinner party in Philadelphia in August 1777. The American general later remarked on "the majesty of his face and his noble and friendly way of greeting officers and citizens alike."

Comte Jean d'Estaing commanded the first French fleet sent to support the American colonists. Inexperienced in naval warfare, he failed to defeat the smaller British fleets along the Atlantic coast and returned to France after an unsuccessful attack off Georgia.

Out of respect for George Washington, whose home was at Mount Vernon, Virginia, and who had served in the Virginia House of Burgesses from 1759 to 1774, Lafayette chose to head a division of Virginians. They proved to be so untrained and ill equipped, barely clothed and shod, that their new general decided to buy them clothes and boots at his own expense (a gesture unheard of in America but common in France) and to drill them daily in preparation for the spring offensive. After the terribly severe winter endured by the troops in Valley Forge — the main camp of the Continental army from December 1777 to June 1778 — good news was desperately needed. France was to provide it.

In January 1778, King Louis XVI recognized American independence, after which Admiral Jean d'Estaing sailed for America with a fleet of ships, bringing much-needed men, arms, and supplies. When the vessels were sighted off the eastern seaboard in May, celebrations were many and Lafayette was publicly credited for having brought about this Franco-American alliance.

The French navy, however, missed opportunities to destroy part or all of the British fleet as it sailed out of Philadelphia and out of Newport, Rhode Island. Lafayette was asked to criticize d'Estaing's conduct, which he refused to do. As a matter of fact, the marquis now saw his role more and more as diplomatic troubleshooter between the two allies. The French and the Americans, with their various vanities and ambitions, were difficult to deal with, however.

Meanwhile, Lafayette had been entrusted with an important task — to inflict great harm to the left wing of General Clinton's army as the British moved up from Philadelphia to New York. This he accomplished splendidly during the Battle of Monmouth Court House (June 28, 1778), even though this minor victory meant little more than better morale among Americans. Lafayette believed that he could do more good for the American cause by persuading France to attack the British either in England or, indirectly, in Canada. He would, of course, want to be at the forefront of such a campaign.

On October 21, 1778, Congress granted Lafayette leave to return home, sent Louis XVI a letter praising the young commander's contribution and service, and asked Dr. Benjamin Franklin, the new ambassador to France, to present the marquis with "an elegant sword with proper devices." The ship *Alliance*, again aptly named, was put at his disposal. Before he sailed for home, Lafayette wrote a touching farewell note in English to George Washington: "I hope your French friend will ever be dear to you, I hope I shall soon see you again, and tell you myself with what affection and respect I'll for ever be, my dear general, your respectful and sincere friend."

The *Alliance* arrived at the port of Brest, in northwestern France, on February 6, 1779, after a very eventful crossing that included a terrific storm off Newfoundland and an attempted mutiny by English deserters and prisoners who had been pressed into naval service. Cheering crowds gave Lafayette a triumphant welcome all along the route that took him from Brest to Versailles. His first duty was to report to Count de Maurepas, the prime minister,

> *He possesses a large share of bravery and military ardor.*
> —GENERAL GEORGE WASHINGTON
> on Lafayette

Benjamin Franklin was sent to the court of Louis XVI in 1776 to obtain economic and military assistance from France. He soon became a hero of the French people, who saw in him the unsophisticated nobility of the New World.

about the situation in the United States and Franco-American strategy. Only then did Lafayette think he could return home to his wife. After such a long separation, Adrienne was ecstatic at seeing him again, and they talked far into the night of his adventures in the New World, about the premature death of their daughter Henriette, and about the infant Anastasie.

Everywhere the couple went, whether in the halls of Versailles or on the streets of Paris, Lafayette was the object of adulation. King Louis XVI allowed him to purchase (for $400,000) a colonel's commission in the King's Dragoons — a position more in keeping with his American standing. Important courtiers listened to his assessment of the Americans' chances for victory over the British. Poets composed verses about his exploits. Countess Aglaé d'Hunolstein, the court beauty who had earlier rejected him, was now more than willing to accept his advances, and for a time she was his mistress.

Lafayette was still the same loving and caring man; now, however, he had acquired maturity and self-confidence, which showed in his easy manner and speech. Before his stay in America many thought him an ungraceful oaf who was perhaps even a little stupid. In the course of all his conversations with Washington, Alexander Hamilton (Washington's aide and treasury secretary), Thomas Jefferson, the Adamses, and others, Lafayette had gradually become more polished. Through his contacts with his soldiers he had learned the art of command and, especially, how to gain their respect.

Adrienne, too, admired the fine qualities her husband had acquired, although she had known all along that "he was the most distinguished, the most amiable person in the world." On Christmas Eve 1779, they had a baby boy whom they christened George Washington de Lafayette, much to the godfather's pleasure.

Lafayette's campaign for an invasion of England came to nothing. However, with the help of the French foreign minister and of Benjamin Franklin, he persuaded his country to support American fighting with sufficient troops and material to win decisively. The French agreed to send 6 ships under Admiral de Termay and 6,000 men under the able command of Lieutenant General the Count de Rochambeau, a seasoned veteran. Lafayette was to be restored to his American rank and to prepare for the arrival of the expeditionary force. After official leave-taking from the king and queen, who wished him well, and from Adrienne, who was quickly discovering the heartaches of being a soldier's wife, Lafayette sailed again for America.

What a difference between his two departures! Three years before, he had left France illegally and incurred the king's anger; now admired and consulted by ministers and generals, he was an official representative of Louis XVI, embarked on an important mission that could only bring honor and glory to his two countries—and indirectly, of course, to himself. When Lafayette stepped onto the docks at Boston Harbor on April 28, 1780, he received a deafening welcome: Guns fired, bells rang, bands marched and played, and crowds cheered.

Washington and French Lieutenant General de Rochambeau prepare to negotiate with British general George Cornwallis. Rochambeau commanded the 6,000 French troops sent to aid the American forces.

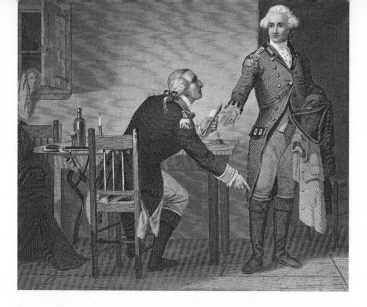

Traitor Benedict Arnold persuades British major John André to smuggle military intelligence in his boot. The papers contained details of a plot by Arnold, a high-ranking American general, to surrender his post at West Point in exchange for £20,000.

The long-heralded French help, which finally arrived in early July, could not have come at a better moment. The American forces lacked everything, from clothes and boots to weapons and ammunition. Lafayette wanted to rejoin Washington as soon as possible and met with him in Morristown, New Jersey, to brief him (and later Congress) on the latest developments. General Lafayette was put in command of the Light Division, 2,300 men (infantry and cavalry) whom he again clothed at his own expense and drilled until they became an elite unit renowned for its spirit.

Meanwhile, the two enemy armies seemed to be engaged in cat-and-mouse pursuits, and very little fighting was actually taking place. Washington and Rochambeau wanted to deal a crushing blow to the British in New York but were waiting for reinforcements. The French fleet, stationed in Rhode Island, interfered with passage to and from England, while Admiral François de Grasse patrolled the American coast with his ships.

In March 1781, Lafayette went to Virginia to pursue the American turncoat Benedict Arnold, now a newly promoted British general. When the traitor escaped, Lafayette was sent to assist General Nathanael Greene in his fight against the forces of the British general George Cornwallis. Their combined forces were no match for Cornwallis's superior numbers, however. The situation was so grave that gloating Cornwallis wrote of Lafayette to his superiors:

"The boy can not escape me." Escape "the boy" did, however, thanks to the arrival of General Anthony Wayne. Lafayette now moved up and down Virginia roads, engaging in various skirmishes and complaining that he was too far away from New York, where the main action was about to take place. Yet he kept harassing Cornwallis and, above all, prevented him from escaping south to the Carolinas.

Cornwallis had been ordered to control the line between Richmond, the capital of Virginia, and Hampton, at the mouth of Chesapeake Bay. When he settled in Yorktown, a fortified town on the York River in Pennsylvania, about 20 miles west of Hampton, Cornwallis realized he had made a terrible blunder. Fresh from a successful encounter with the English navy, Admiral de Grasse was arriving at full speed with a fleet of 24 warships, 1,788 guns, and more than 3,000 men and would block any escape or rescue by sea.

When de Grasse's French marines landed and joined Lafayette's unit on September 5, 1781, Washington was so overjoyed that he announced in his general orders: "As no circumstance could possibly have happened more opportunely in point of time, no prospect could ever have promised more important successes, and nothing but our want of exertions can probably blast the pleasing prospects before us." The commander in chief was right: Cornwallis was trapped.

The Treaty of Commerce and Alliance was signed by Benjamin Franklin (center) and French delegates in 1778. In the treaty, France agreed to provide the colonies with substantial loans and military assistance.

Wisely and tactfully postponing a direct attack on Yorktown, Lafayette tightened his vise around the town and waited for his two allied superiors, Washington and Rochambeau, to approach from the New York area. They arrived in force and laid siege to the city, while Lafayette was entrusted with the important mission of capturing English redoubts, or small fortifications. With courage and renewed vigor, his American soldiers coolly braved cannon and musket fire, using only their fixed bayonets in their charge up enemy positions. After several hours of furious battle "the boy" won a strategic victory and dealt a severe blow to Cornwallis.

In a desperate move, the English tried to force their way out but were easily thrown back. Their

Cornwallis surrenders the British troops to Washington and Rochambeau after his decisive defeat at the Battle of Yorktown on October 19, 1781. Although Yorktown was the last major battle of the war, it would be two years before the Treaty of Paris was signed in 1783.

situation was by then hopeless, and soon after they asked for a cease-fire, which was refused: Only unconditional surrender would be accepted. This they finally signed on October 19, 1781. Ironically, English redcoats and German mercenaries laid down their arms as their own marching band played "The World Turn'd Upside Down." Lafayette's fifes and drums added a jubilant "Yankee Doodle Dandy." Victory was so very sweet!

The next day, in his report to the French prime minister, the marquis wrote that the fifth act of the play was over. Indeed, for all intents and purposes, the war was over: The British resolve had been broken, and within two years a peace treaty would be signed.

3

Hero of Two Worlds

While he was preparing to return home, Gilbert de Lafayette received word that he had been promoted to *maréchal de camp* (brigadier general) in the French army. In all the towns he passed through on his way to Boston, from which he would sail for France, he was the object of grateful ovations and celebrations.

After arriving in the northwestern French port of L'Orient on January 17, 1782, Lafayette rode directly to Paris, where crowds cheered the brave nobleman. The king and queen bestowed numerous medals on the marquis, dinners were given in his honor, and he delivered speeches to learned societies. During a performance of Christoph Gluck's opera *Iphigénie en Aulide*, attended by the Lafayettes, the entire house broke into wild applause when the chorus began the aria "Achilles is crowned by Victory's hands." (Achilles was a legendary Greek warrior-hero.) All the newspapers were praising the marquis and calling him the "Hero of Two Worlds."

There was a universal sentiment of regret at his departure, accompanied with a cordial and unanimous approval of the motive and spirit by which he was actuated.
—WILLIAM CUTTER
historian, on Lafayette's leaving America

The ruling class attends the Paris opera. Following his return to France in January 1782, Lafayette resumed the habits of his aristocratic station, attending formal dinner parties, concerts, and the opera. During one operatic performance, the entire audience applauded Lafayette as France's newfound hero.

Prussian king Frederick the Great dines with friends in his opulent palace, Sans Souci, near Berlin. A self-proclaimed champion of free speech, Frederick held heated discussions at the palace with many writers and scholars, including the French philosopher Voltaire, seated at right.

Lafayette seized the opportunity provided by his fame to work on behalf of the United States — at times, some thought, to the detriment of French interests. In his new, official capacity as special adviser to American representatives in Paris, he took on Louis XVI's ministries with the same tireless energy and determination he used to extract supplies, arms, or men during his American campaign. For instance, he obtained numerous commercial and financial advantages for the United States — such as duty-free ports, reduced customs duties, and preferential terms. He also successfully negotiated a 6-million-livres loan for the Americans, thereby gaining the U.S. Treasury Department's undying gratitude.

The new maréchal de camp was also pressing Count de Vergennes, the French foreign minister, and Count de Ségur, the war minister, to continue the war on England. They finally agreed and planned to attack, with Spain, the West Indies. A naval force had in fact been gathered in Cadiz, Spain, under d'Estaing's command, and Lafayette joined it late in 1782. However, the war ended in early January 1783 when a preliminary armistice was signed between the independent United States and Britain.

The freedoms guaranteed by the Declaration of Independence did not extend to the American slaves, who were brought from Africa and sold at auctions such as this one in Virginia. Both Thomas Jefferson and George Washington were slave owners.

Adrienne remained a loyal and loving wife to Lafayette, despite his numerous affairs during the couple's 34-year marriage. Lafayette later wrote, "Her tenderness, her kindness, the elevation, the dedicatedness, the generosity of her soul charmed, embellished, and honored my life."

Two amusing stories are told about Lafayette and a couple of particularly conservative kings. To reward Lafayette for all his glorious deeds, some proposed that if Jamaica was captured from the English, the marquis should be made governor. The king of Spain supposedly rejected the idea with horror, saying, "Never! He would create a republic there!" Another story about Lafayette's political beliefs involved Frederick the Great. In 1785, the marquis attended Prussian army maneuvers at the king's invitation. One evening, after Gilbert de Lafayette had affirmed that the United States would never have kings or aristocrats, Frederick reportedly said to him: "I once knew a young man who, having visited countries where liberty and equality were the rule, then decided to defend these principles in his own country. Do you know what happened to him?"

"No, sire," Lafayette answered.

"Well, sir," Frederick is said to have replied, "he was hanged."

That he was considered an antiroyalist and a republican, albeit by very reactionary monarchs, was an interesting notion. Of course, Lafayette had had long discussions with American leaders, both in France and in the United States, about representative government at the state and national levels. George Washington, whom he loved and admired, had convinced him of the need for freedom of the press, of assembly, and of religion. In fact, Lafayette went even further in his thinking: He proposed that he and Washington buy land together, free the slaves, and employ them as tenant farmers. Such emancipation would set a fine example for the West Indies and the American South.

Washington, a slave owner, never responded to this partnership idea, but Lafayette did purchase a plantation in Latin America and gradually freed his slaves, who were then, as planned, employed as tenant farmers. Other social reforms included helping Protestant communities of his native province of Auvergne regain some of the rights they had lost under Louis XIV, founding a school for the children of Chavaniac, and helping to establish a new wool-weaving factory.

Only Lafayette could always reach both King and government, only he could plead shamelessly and endlessly for the American cause: he had, in fact, become an irreplaceable liaison.
—OLIVIER BERNIER
historian, on Lafayette's peacetime diplomatic role

A miniature of Adrienne (left) is displayed next to a portrait of her three children, Anastasie, George Washington, and Virginie, who are standing around a bust of their father, Lafayette. Adrienne was left to manage the household for years at a time while her husband fought his battles.

Lafayette's private life was also busy. His wife adored him more than ever; in September 1782 she bore another daughter, whom they named Virginie in honor of Washington's birthplace. Aglaé d'Hunolstein was completely smitten with the "Hero of Two Worlds," but he had fallen in love with another young woman at the French court, Diane de Simiane, with whom he would carry on a lasting relationship. Finally, although Lafayette had spent the enormous sum of 700,000 livres ($3,500,000) on the American war, he was still a very wealthy man, with an annual income of roughly 130,000 livres.

The Marquis and Marquise de Lafayette and their three children moved into a beautiful mansion on rue de Bourbon (today, rue de Lille), across from the famous Tuileries Gardens. Their home quickly became a center of liberal thought and a "must-stop" for all foreign dignitaries. Typical conversations concerned the best form of government, elected representation, civil rights, free trade, and the deteriorating French economy.

Personal and public adulation notwithstanding, Lafayette was restless, and he yearned for the intoxicating excitement he had felt in America. When George Washington, who had retired to Mount Vernon, invited him for a long visit, Lafayette jumped at the opportunity. He arrived in New York on the evening of August 4, 1784, and was greeted by jubilant crowds. For the returning hero and "Liberator of America," four months of euphoria had begun.

George Washington stands with Lafayette on the terrace of his home at Mount Vernon. Lafayette spent two weeks there in 1784, discussing the importance of strong central government.

4

Champion of the Nation

July 14, 1789, marked a turning point in the history of France. The urgency of the country's severe political and economic crises aroused the spirit of revolution. The people of Paris marched on the Bastille prison, merciless in their rage. They lynched and beheaded various officials and profiteers and later razed the tower.

Measures had to be taken quickly to restore order. Lafayette and several other deputies agreed to proceed from Versailles to the capital. In Paris, Lafayette addressed and calmed huge crowds and in the process was named by acclamation to the rank of commandant-general of the Paris National Guard. He then swore to sacrifice his life to preserve the people's liberty.

Within a few days, King Louis XVI arrived in the city from Versailles escorted by 100,000 militiamen.

Your majesty knows my devotion to the Crown, but if it separates itself from the cause of the people, I shall remain on the side of the people.
—MARQUIS DE LAFAYETTE
to Louis XVI after
returning from Varennes

Lafayette holds a copy of his "Declaration of the Rights of Man and Citizen," which he presented to the National Assembly in 1789. Modeled after the American Declaration of Independence, the document declared all men free and equal at birth.

On July 14, 1789, thousands of angry Parisians stormed the Bastille prison, which had come to symbolize the hated monarchy. The date is still celebrated as the anniversary of the French Revolution and the birth of a new republic.

General Lafayette, who wanted to grant more power to the people while preserving the monarchy, formally presented the king to the Parisians and placed him under his and the Guard's protection. Lafayette even went so far as to pin the white cockade of monarchy onto the blue and red colors of the City of Paris. In this attempt at reconciling these two inimical forces — the tradition-bound, reactionary regime and the vibrant, often unruly mobs — the Marquis had created a brand-new symbol of France —the tricolor flag.

In order to help resolve the financial and monetary crisis facing the kingdom, Louis XVI and Loménie de Brienne, his chief minister, had finally convened a meeting of the Estates-General (the National Assembly). As a delegate from his province of Auvergne, in central France, Lafayette had been elected to this body. Its mission was to reverse the effects of more than a hundred years of absolute rule and exorbitant spending, which had brought France to the brink of total bankruptcy.

The government's ineffectual economic policies — which consisted of borrowing instead of taxing and spending instead of saving — had resulted in budget deficits, higher inflation and interest rates, and unemployment. Caught in a vicious circle, the king appointed and dismissed in very short order a succession of finance ministers.

At the same time, a series of crop failures had caused the price of bread and other staples to rise even further. As terrible hardships loomed for the lower and middle classes, they were outraged by the moral corruption and ostentatious luxury and waste of the privileged sectors, and especially by scandals involving Queen Marie Antoinette and her entourage.

The upper classes, comprised of churchmen (the First Estate) and nobles (the Second Estate), were unwilling to give up their privileges, however, particularly their tax exemption. The bourgeoisie, or middle class (the Third Estate), wanted to gain various legal rights if they were to support any new taxes to eliminate the budget deficit. At last, after eight long months of preparation and behind-the-scenes maneuvers, a meeting began on May 5, 1789, at the magnificent Palace of Versailles, southwest of Paris, with the king and queen in attendance.

Forced out of their usual meeting hall in Versailles, members of the National Assembly met in a nearby tennis court. There they took the so-called Jeu de Paume or Tennis Court Oath, vowing never to disband until a written constitution had been established for France.

Hungry peasants, most of them women, marched to Versailles to demand that Louis XVI abolish feudal privileges and accept the Declaration of Rights. They stormed the palace and forced the royal family to return to Paris.

Despite the splendid costumes and all the pomp and circumstance, there were problems from the start. For one thing, Lafayette felt duty-bound to vote with the nobility bloc rather than with the Third Estate, with which his ideas were more in tune. For another, reactionary factions realized that the convening of the Estates-General had set the stage for a power struggle and had been a big blunder; they wanted a return to the status quo.

When Louis XVI dismissed his finance minister, Jacques Necker, and unwisely ordered the hall locked, the Third Estate representatives — along with a few liberals from the other groups (sometimes called the "Americans") — responded angrily. They defiantly moved to the Salle du Jeu de Paume (the indoor tennis court) and swore to remain there as a duly elected National Assembly. No doubt encouraged by American principles of democracy and by the U.S. Constitution, newly framed and approved in Philadelphia, the French deputies began to work on a constitution of their own, one that would spell out the duties and prerogatives of the people, the Crown, and the Estates-General. The king now relented and allowed all three groups to deliberate together as equals.

Gilbert de Lafayette had written to President George Washington on January 1, 1788, to congratulate him on the new American Constitution and had pointedly noted that a Bill of Rights ought to be added in order to make the document a perfect instrument of governance. On July 11, 1789, Lafayette presented to his colleagues of the Constituent Assembly a "Declaration of the Rights of Man and Citizen," which he had been writing since the beginning of that year. The result of his discussions with Thomas Jefferson, then American ambassador to France, who praised and recommended it to his friend James Madison (who would become the fourth president of the United States), this draft embodied in nine short paragraphs the principles Lafayette cherished most: liberty, equality, justice for all, inalienable rights, and sovereignty of the nation. Calling it his "profession of faith, fruit of my past, pledge of my future" as well as "a manifesto and an ultimatum," he received such an enthusiastic response from the assemblymen that they elected him their vice-president. The text of his declaration was soon after revised and improved and serves to this day as the preamble to the French constitution.

Georges-Jacques Danton was the founder of the outlawed Club des Cordeliers and a prominent leader in the French Revolution. He later became the first president of the Committee of Public Safety, the executive branch of France's revolutionary government.

Maximilien Robespierre was the leader of the Jacobin faction and a tyrannical force in the revolutionary government. A fierce opponent of Lafayette's, he accused the general of trying to establish a military dictatorship.

In less than a week, the Marquis de Lafayette, descendant of one of the most aristocratic houses of France, had, ironically, helped abolish absolute rule and become an important leader of the Revolution in his dual role as commandant-general of the Paris National Guard and vice-president of the National Assembly. Faced with open hostility, Louis XVI was again forced to obey the majority's will. Nevertheless, the atmosphere was rife with rumors that the king and the privileged class planned to seize power again, and these rumors fueled disturbances all over France. In Paris, General de Lafayette, mounted on his white stallion, successfully defused several disturbances. However, as food supplies dwindled, rioting broke out. On October 5, 1789, a large group consisting mainly of women, soon joined by unemployed workers, marched on Versailles to demand that Louis XVI sign the abolition of feudal privileges and accept the Declaration of the Rights of Man and Citizen.

When the crowds did not disperse as Lafayette expected, he and his troops rushed to the palace in order to protect both the king and the Assembly. Anxious to prevent mob rule and total anarchy, the general proposed to place the royal family under the protection of the National Guard to move them to the capital, and immediately to give the masses bread for the coming winter. After demonstrators entered the palace and killed several bodyguards, Lafayette was finally able to reestablish order by appearing on the main balcony with the king, queen, and dauphin (the eldest son of the French king) in a symbolic gesture of national reconciliation. On the evening of October 6, the family and their courtiers moved to the Tuileries Palace in Paris, under Lafayette's personal guarantee of safety. The National Assembly reconvened on October 19; Lafayette had for the moment averted civil war.

In addition to working for improved political conditions in the kingdom, the general completely reorganized the National Guard. Although many suspected him of considering the use of force to become a dictator, Lafayette, like his mentor, George Washington, believed that the military was subordinate to civilian authority. Uninterested in personal power, he believed his duty entailed not

On July 14, 1790, Lafayette and the National Guard marched down the Champ-de-Mars to celebrate the first anniversary of the fall of the Bastille. On a grand altar Lafayette swore "to be ever faithful to the Nation, the Laws, and the King."

Louis XVI and the royal family, disguised as servants, were captured near Varennes on June 21, 1791, during their attempt to flee the kingdom. Louis had hoped to escape to Austria and seek aid from his brother-in-law, the Habsburg emperor.

only foiling the plots of royalists, who favored monarchical government, but also keeping in check the increasingly virulent "clubs," or debating societies (groups that gained power by appealing to prejudice and making false promises). The most vicious of all were the Clubs des Cordeliers and des Jacobins, so named because they met, respectively, in former convents of the Franciscan and Jacobin orders. Their leaders included such firebrand revolutionaries as the pamphleteer Jean-Paul Marat (later stabbed to death in his bath by Charlotte Corday) and the lawyers Georges-Jacques Danton and Maximilien Robespierre (both guillotined in 1794).

At this time Lafayette was attacked both by the royal court and the demagogic clubs. The court considered him a traitor to its cause; the clubs thought he had royalist leanings. Nevertheless, Lafayette began preparations for a gigantic festival on July 14, 1790, to celebrate the first anniversary of the taking of the Bastille. The city of Paris had invited representatives to gather there for a great federation; Lafayette and his troops then took a solemn oath of loyalty to "Nation, Law and King" and were cheered by some 15,000 delegates and 300,000 spectators gathered on the Champ-de-Mars (where the Eiffel Tower stands today). In his memoirs Lafayette called the festivities "one of the greatest events of the Revolution" and wrote that he hoped that they marked "the birth of public peace and happiness."

Despite these heartfelt sentiments and Louis XVI's cooperation, tensions between the people of Paris and the court continued to grow because of Lafayette's harshness and inflexibility in repressing both royalist and popular riots and demonstrations. More and more, his guardsmen refused to obey his orders and sometimes went as far as insulting him in front of jeering crowds; in response, he resigned his command in April 1791. Only when a delegation begged him to reconsider, swearing anew to obey the law and punish the rebellious militiamen, did he return to his post.

The royal family was brought back to Paris along a route lined with soldiers and guardsmen. They were received at the Tuileries Palace amid deathly silence, in what was described as "the funeral procession of the monarchy."

When celebrations at the second anniversary of the Bastille turned into a riot, Lafayette ordered the National Guard to open fire. Some 50 people were killed and scores of others were wounded in an incident that destroyed Lafayette's popularity with the working classes.

In the meantime, Louis XVI realized that he was now a prisoner of the Assembly and the radical clubs, unable to travel as he pleased, his loyalty to the new order constantly questioned. Hopeful that his brother-in-law, the Austrian emperor, would help him regain his throne, Louis decided to flee his kingdom. Traveling with false passports and disguised as domestics, he, his family, and his most faithful retainers made a rush for the eastern frontier during the night of June 20–21, 1791.

The king's plan was simple enough: At army headquarters in Metz he would meet with General Marquis de Bouillé and lead a popular uprising against the Paris government. To further ensure his success, influential émigrés, men and women who had escaped France at the beginning of the Revolution (his two brothers were among them), would rally around the monarch.

Finally, Louis XVI intended to convince his foreign allies (mainly Austrians and Prussians) to invade France and help him destroy the constitutional

government and reestablish the old monarchy. However, at a small relay station not far from the village of Varennes, the innkeeper recognized the monarch's face from coins and alerted the local authorities, who immediately arrested the royal party — an act that moved Louis XVI to declare, "There is no more king in France."

That same morning, June 21, an angry National Assembly suspended all the king's functions, closed France's borders, and raised a volunteer force of 10,000. The deputies also accused Lafayette either of complicity or stupidity. Club leader Danton expressed very well the fury of his fellow Cordeliers when he demanded prompt punishment: "The commandant-general [Lafayette] promised on his head that the king would not leave; we must have the person of the king or the head of the commandant-general!"

The slow return to Paris, along a route lined with soldiers and guardsmen, was a humiliating ordeal for Louis XVI and Marie Antoinette. Although Lafayette had given strict orders to safeguard the royal personages, the troops could not — or preferred not to — prevent insults, threats, and minor scuffles from occurring. Once in Paris, the reception turned icy cold, for the National Guard had been issued the order of the day, "No shout, no salute." It was in this terrible silence that the king and his family reentered the Tuileries Palace. Now, under constant watch, they were prisoners indeed.

During the second celebration of Bastille Day, certain Jacobins and Cordeliers drafted a petition demanding that the king be deposed; another petition called for his trial. A riot ensued, which required Paris mayor Jean-Sylvain Bailly to declare martial law; when the mob refused to disperse and started to hurl rocks at the Guard and its general, the troops overreacted and opened fire, killing about 50 people and wounding scores of others. The Champ-de-Mars Affair, as it became known, destroyed Lafayette's popularity with the Parisian working classes and any remaining influence he might still have had with the clubs.

Despite countless threats along the route, the royal family arrived safely at Paris's Tuileries Palace. Though the Constituent Assembly agreed to be part of the king's entourage, 300 of its upper-class members resigned rather than have to face the enraged Parisian masses.

The royal family watches in horror from inside the palace while crowds riot below.

In spite of these setbacks, Lafayette, who believed the country was not yet ready for a republican government, tried to save the constitutional monarchy he had worked so hard to establish. Moderate members of the Assembly did finally write a document, which Louis XVI accepted and swore to uphold on September 14, 1791. The happy event was celebrated all over France, and at Lafayette's urging a general amnesty for political prisoners was enthusiastically approved. The commandant-general could now satisfy his wife's wishes by resigning his commission and returning to his home in Auvergne. Full of optimism, he declared in his farewell address to his troops that "the days of the revolution have given way to a regular organization, to liberty and the prosperity which it guarantees."

In fact, the situation was catastrophic, because power no longer rested with the king or the newly elected Legislative Assembly but with the extreme-left clubs. "Organized" mob rule had replaced law and order, and the monarchy was rendered totally ineffective. Many believed that only war could save the king; at the same time, the radical Jacobins

hoped the approaching conflict would instill renewed patriotic fervor in the citizenry. War fever spread, and a pretext was quickly found: France demanded her émigrés' immediate return from Austria. Increasingly harsher notes were exchanged between Paris and Vienna, leading to a declaration of war on April 20, 1792. The French Revolutionary Wars — hostilities between France and various European powers during the period 1792–1802 — had begun. The French army, however, was nowhere near ready for battle and at first appeared to be on the verge of defeat.

General de Lafayette was recalled from retirement and named commander of the Army of the Center, over the Jacobins' violent opposition. To Lafayette's horror, Louis XVI was stripped more and more of his constitutional prerogatives. Stationed in Metz, far from the capital, the general found himself un-

On July 12, 1789, a group of radicals joined by workers and students invaded the Tuileries Palace and overthrew the king. Declared a traitor and threatened with arrest, Lafayette sought to escape the turmoil by emigrating to Belgium.

able to mount a counterrebellion against the extremist Jacobin Robespierre and his followers, whose supremacy in the Assembly, the provincial clubs, and the Paris neighborhoods was now uncontested. When he then learned that he had been proscribed and his properties confiscated ("Strike Lafayette, and the nation is safe," Robespierre had thundered), he and a small group of friendly officers crossed the frontier on August 19, 1792, into neutral Belgium, from which they would sail to safety in the United States.

Naively, Lafayette requested safe passage through Austrian lines. Instead, he was arrested by General Moitelle in the name of monarchists everywhere. The marquis and three of his companions were banished to the fortress of Wesel in Westphalia (a region in present-day West Germany). Thus began the long and terrible years of imprisonment.

5

The Terrible Years

Once called the "Hero of Two Worlds," the "Liberator of America," and the "George Washington of France," General de Lafayette had become the pariah of Europe. To the royalists he was a bloodthirsty traitor who had been solely responsible for the Revolution and had sold the king to the mob; to the revolutionaries he was a lukewarm patriot more interested in his own fame than in political reform; to the European monarchs he represented the worst example of change and a threat to their own crowns. Everyone wanted him kept in prison, and if he were to die there, few would shed a tear.

At the fortress of Wesel, Lafayette and his three loyal companions were given substandard food, were allowed no physical exercise, and received no medical care. Lafayette's health deteriorated, and he began to suffer from migraine headaches, sleeplessness, and chest pains. He could have received better treatment, however, had he been willing to reveal the plans and strength of the French army stationed on France's eastern border. When Lafayette heard this outrageous proposition, he rejected it indignantly, believing it beneath both him and King Frederick William II, who had suggested the bargain.

The aristocracy and despotism are in their death throes. My blood, crying vengeance, will provide new defenders for liberty.
—MARQUIS DE LAFAYETTE
after his arrest

On his way to Belgium, Lafayette was captured by Austrian guards and imprisoned in Westphalia. Although he had fled France because of his loyalty to the king, in the rest of Europe he was considered a dangerous revolutionary.

The French revolutionary army defeated Prussian forces on September 20, 1792, at the Battle of Valmy. Their victory, however, meant greater hardship for Lafayette, who was imprisoned in Prussia at the time.

Fortunately, Lafayette was allowed to write to his wife and friends through émigré intermediaries, using the margins of book pages for writing paper and a pin dipped in mud for pen and ink. But his situation soon worsened. When the Prussians were defeated at Valmy on September 20, 1792, and the Republic was proclaimed the next day, harsher measures were taken against Lafayette and his party. At the end of the year they were moved to Magdeburg, a fortress in the heart of Saxony, where prison life became even more severe and vindictive.

Using a toothpick dipped in his own blood, Lafayette wrote a letter to a lady friend in London and smuggled it out with the help of a guard he had bribed. In the letter, Lafayette described his exis-

tence in a matter-of-fact and sometimes ironic style: "After successively opening four sets of doors, each armed with chains, padlocks, iron bars, one reaches, not without trouble or noise, my cell which is three steps wide and five steps long. It is dark and damp. . . . My health worsens daily, but I am set on living." Through the grapevine he learned of French victories, of the guillotining of Louis XVI and Marie Antoinette, of the beginning of the Reign of Terror in France, when some 2,500 alleged counterrevolutionaries were brought to the guillotine, and of his family's situation.

Adrienne had courageously defended the family honor and properties after her husband's supposed "desertion" and the condemnation by Robespierre

The executioner displays the head of Louis XVI to the crowd of citizens and soldiers who had come to witness his death. His execution on January 21, 1793, provoked war between France and the surrounding monarchies in Europe and ignited the counterrevolutionary movement in France.

and his Jacobin colleagues, now in full charge of the country. Many aristocrats and moderates were being sent daily to die, and at first it was thanks to the Lafayettes' past goodness and generosity that they were able to reside at Chavaniac, though on parole. Yet the Committee of Public Safety, as the dictatorial governing body was called, continued to resent the presence of the young woman and her family, and in November 1793, Adrienne was imprisoned.

Gouverneur Morris, the American ambassador, made it clear to the French, however, that the United States held the Lafayettes very dear and that if harm came to them Franco-American relations would be severely damaged. Because France was then politically isolated in Europe, no further action was taken against the young woman. Then, in that same summer of 1794, the Reign of Terror and the killings ended with the fall and execution of Robespierre, though the change came too late for Adrienne's grandmother, mother, and oldest sister: They had been beheaded a week earlier. Mme. de Lafayette was freed six months later, on January 21, 1795. Frail and ill, she moved in with the James Monroes (he was the new American ambassador), who offered to nurse her back to health.

Adrienne's only worry became her husband and his release. Lafayette and his friends had been moved about and finally put in prison in the fortress of Olmutz, in what today is Czechoslovakia. While Lafayette had borne his previous painful incarceration with spirit, he was now to endure much more. Placed in solitary confinement, he was denied everything except the barest of necessities. Such physical and mental deprivation (he no longer had a name, but was simply called Prisoner No. 2) made him so ill that the Austrian government relented in its barbarism and allowed him some exercise. Under his guards' watchful eye, he could go for walks in the neighboring woods. He could also plan his escape.

With the help of a bribed jailer, Lafayette had been secretly corresponding with two men — one the son of the very same South Carolina plantation owner with whom he had stayed on his first night in America in 1777. Both had arranged for an escape on November 8, 1794, buying horses and hiding clothes and money. During his usual walk that morning, Lafayette managed to break away from his escort, who bit the end of the prisoner's finger off in the process and ran to give the alarm.

On October 14, 1793, Marie-Antoinette was summoned from her solitary confinement in the Conciergerie to appear before the Revolutionary Tribunal. The hated queen was guillotined two days later.

Unfortunately, he was eventually captured and returned the next day to the fortress. His accomplices were condemned to six months at hard labor, but Lafayette was more severely punished. All physical activity was denied, no one was allowed to speak to him, and no communication to or from the prisoner was permitted. Under pressure from some cabinet members, the emperor countermanded an order to put him in chains.

Although the escape attempt had disastrous consequences for Lafayette, it also served to rally support for his liberation, particularly in the United States, Holland, Sweden, and England. Above all, the attempt informed Adrienne that her husband was still alive and in Austrian custody. As head of the Lafayette family, she undertook, therefore, to work on Gilbert's behalf. With the help of Ambassador Monroe, she obtained American passports in the name of Motier and, having sent her teenage son to Mount Vernon, boarded a New York-bound ship that made an unexpected stop at Hamburg. "Mrs. Motier" and her two daughters, citizens from Hartford, Connecticut, were the only three passengers to debark in that German port.

Prisoners await their fate during the "Reign of Terror" (1793–94). The revolutionary government imprisoned hundreds of thousands of suspected enemies and executed some 17,000 — including the grandmother, mother, and sister of Lafayette's wife.

By all accounts, Adrienne was an extraordinary woman, fiercely devoted to her husband (both the man and his ideas) despite his flaws and infidelities. Before the Revolution, she had managed the family affairs during the general's long and frequent absences and raised their three children herself. When Lafayette was imprisoned, she had to be even more watchful over the family's interests and good name. In prison, she had acquired a mental toughness in order to survive her 14-month ordeal. It was no wonder, then, that when Adrienne saw an aunt, Mme. de Tessé, in Hamburg, her relative found her changed — but also could discern in her niece "a surprising calm and a resolute air which had something imposing." Adrienne would soon draw on all these qualities in order to accomplish her mission.

Mme. de Lafayette had quite simply decided, with permission from Emperor Francis II, to join her husband in prison and to share his abject treatment. She, Anastasie, and Virginie arrived at Olmutz on October 15, 1795, and were immediately taken to the marquis's cell. The four inmates looked at one another in surprise. Lafayette had aged 20 years and looked like a skeleton; Adrienne was thin, her hair almost gray; the two girls had matured. But the joy of the reunion somehow lessened their shock as they embraced and kissed, overjoyed to find one another alive.

Although Adrienne and her daughters had entered the prison voluntarily, they were subjected to the same frightful conditions as the other prisoners, except that they remained together for most of the day, reading aloud, telling stories of the outside world, and watching Virginie, a born mimic, make fun of the Olmutz staff. In addition to these activities, Mme. de Lafayette wrote letters and a biography of her mother, who had been a wonderful *grande dame* of the Ancien Régime (as pre-Revolution France was called) and had taught her so well the value of service, honor, and heroism.

Food, which was now in adequate supply, because they paid for it, was "indescribably filthy." Thanks to a relatively better diet and, above all, to his loved

> *Their meeting, who shall attempt to describe! One moment, the heart of the husband and father is fainting under those horrible doubts . . . the next moment, his wife and children rush into his arms, and cover him with kisses and tears.*
> —WILLIAM CUTTER
> historian

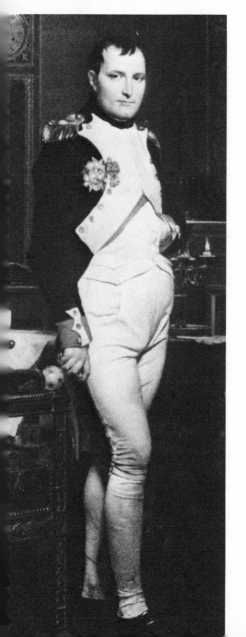

While Lafayette was in prison, another formidable general was rising to power — Napoleon Bonaparte. He commanded the army of Italy in several victorious campaigns in Europe and Africa and returned to France in 1799.

ones' presence, Lafayette's morale and physical well-being improved. His wife's health worsened, however. Adrienne developed headaches, her arms and legs swelled, and she suffered from eczema, an itching, encrusted skin condition. She was granted permission to consult a specialist in Vienna, but only if she never returned to Olmutz. With natural dignity she refused, choosing her suffering over the pain of another separation.

News of the "Martyrs of Olmutz" was circulating on both sides of the Atlantic, and numerous officials began pressuring Austria to free the Lafayettes. Influential journalists were publishing every detail of the Austrians' shameful conduct. President Washington personally appealed to Emperor Francis.

In the meantime, following the fall of Robespierre, a new ruling body, the Directory, had come to power in France, and with it General Napoleon Bonaparte's star had risen. Bonaparte had just inflicted a series of lightning defeats on the supposedly unbeatable Austrian army that forced the Vienna government to sue for peace in the spring of 1797. One of the peace treaty articles dealt with the release of the Lafayettes. Apparently victories on the battlefield could still achieve what lobbying and public opinion had failed to accomplish.

However, two requirements were to delay any action concerning Lafayette. For one, Baron von Thugut, Francis II's chief minister, demanded that Lafayette sign a memorandum promising never to set foot on Austrian soil again. This he refused to do, because he might later be asked to lead a diplomatic mission there — or more likely a military operation. For another, the French Directory wanted Lafayette's freedom as a matter of national honor but was not eager to repatriate a liberal of whose views they were suspicious. Consequently, they had stipulated that he settle anywhere but France, preferably in the faraway United States.

Finally, all was resolved. Von Thugut relented after receiving from the American consul the meaningless assurance that Lafayette would not visit Austria in the near future. More complicated was the question of Lafayette's unofficial exile. Ever

since his defection at Metz in 1792, Lafayette had been on his country's proscribed list, which meant that he still could not go back to France without a pardon. Despite his repeated declarations of loyalty to the new regime and of allegiance to republican principles, Lafayette was not allowed to return home.

On September 19, 1797, the Austrians drove "the whole Lafayette caravan" to Hamburg (after giving them much-needed clothes and shoes), where they officially handed them over to the American consul at Hamburg. They were free at last. Adrienne had sacrificed and suffered much and, in fact, never recovered from her illnesses and ailments. Her two daughters had been just as heroic. Both had endured inhumane treatment for no other reason than their love and devotion to their parents. Anastasie had retained her good looks but was thin and pale; the 15-year-old Virginie, a lively, pleasant girl, had developed a slight stoop from her imprisonment.

Lafayette, who had just turned 40, had been marked by his 5 long years in prison. Though he did not waver from his views on liberty and national will, it was not without a certain disenchantment. "The people's cause is no less sacred to me," he had written in jail. "I would give my blood for it, but the charm is destroyed."

Anastasie rests on her father's knee while Adrienne kneels by his side in their prison cell in Olmutz. Adrienne and her daughters joined Lafayette in prison in October 1795 and remained with him for two years, becoming the martyrs of Europe.

6

Life of a Country Gentleman

Because Lafayette could not yet return to France after his liberation, he and his family settled first in Wittmold, a charming little town on Ploen Lake, where Mme. de Tessé, Adrienne's aunt, had bought a large house surrounded by hills and woods. In this calm, clean air, pampered by all, the Lafayettes tried to recover some of their health. One of Lafayette's first tasks was to write a letter thanking all those who had acted to free him: Major Huger, the plantation owner in South Carolina whose son had unsuccessfully engineered the general's escape; President Washington; General Fitzpatrick and Charles James Fox, who had both eloquently spoken on his behalf in the House of Commons in England; and especially General Napoleon Bonaparte, whose victories had brought Austria to the negotiating table and forced the prisoners' release from Olmutz.

> *Doubtless I've made a lot of mistakes, but that's because I've done a lot.*
> —MARQUIS DE LAFAYETTE

Napoleon strolls with the Austrian archduke at the palace of Würzburg in Franconia. After the defeat of its army in 1805, Austria was forced to cede territory to Napoleon's empire and to grant Napoleon the hand of Archduchess Marie Louise.

Napoleon and his wife Josephine wait in a salon at the Tuileries following the coup d'état of 18 Brumaire, which took place on November 9, 1799. Napoleon overthrew the leaders of the Directory, dispersed the legislative councils, and set up a new consulate under his rule.

In time, Wittmold began to seem too small, so the Lafayettes rented a castle nearby, at Lemkuhlen. It provided not only space but also safety, for it was located in the then-Danish province of Holstein and was thus beyond the reach of the powers united against France. Numerous visitors dropped by to see Lafayette, offer help, and participate in heated discussions of the political situation in France. Rather than look back and regret their past, the entire household was in a state of happy confusion caused by the pregnancy of Adrienne's sister, Pauline de Montagu, and by the approaching marriage between Anastasie and Charles de Latour-Maubourg, the younger brother of Lafayette's fellow prisoner. Adrienne had to be carried into the chapel for the ceremony; Lafayette walked in dressed in a brand-new American general's uniform.

Although the year at Lemkuhlen was one of the family's happiest — Lafayette's son George had even returned from the United States in February 1798 — their financial situation was worsening, because most of their landholdings had been confiscated by the French government during the marquis's imprisonment. Lafayette could not reenter France to try to set things right because he feared arrest, but his wife was not on the list of proscribed citizens.

Adrienne knew from long years of practice how to handle money and could be both firm and tactful in her dealings with government officials. As soon as she was able to travel, therefore, she and Virginie left for Paris. Although she was unable to arrange for the return of the confiscated properties, she made useful contacts and was allowed to "commute" between France and the general's residence. The Lafayettes decided that this meant they could move closer to France; thus, early in 1799, they settled in Vianen, Holland, not far from Utrecht.

Money was still a problem, so the Lafayettes, the Montagus, and the Grammonts (the families of two of the Noailles sisters) rented a large home, which was soon filled with the sound of babies' cries. Adrienne and her sisters divided their inheritance from their mother and grandmother; Adrienne received the château of Lagrange a handsome 14th-century castle 30 miles east of Paris. While Lafayette waited for his wife to win her cause through visits to influential people, he read books on agriculture and animal husbandry. The family was holding its own.

Conditions in France were deteriorating, however, and the ruling Directory members were busier fighting over the spoils of the Revolution than governing. The people, especially small shopkeepers, wanted above all to be rid of chaos and disorder, even at the cost of certain civil rights. General Bonaparte understood the temper of the times better than anyone and knew he had the will to act accordingly. Thus, he returned to France after his inconclusive Egyptian campaign to mount a coup against the Directory, which he did on November 9, 1799. The next day, as first consul, or head of the Consulate, as the new governing body was called,

> *Lafayette may be right in theory; but then, what is a theory?*
> —NAPOLEON BONAPARTE

he declared: "Frenchmen, you will undoubtedly recognize in my conduct the zeal of a soldier of liberty and of a citizen devoted to the Republic."

Lafayette understood the first consul's statement to mean that there was no more proscription and, at Adrienne's urging, rushed back to France, hoping for a political or military role. Instead, Bonaparte was furious and threatened to have him arrested. Finally, in a compromise worked out by Adrienne, Lafayette was given tacit permission to remain as long as he avoided public life. Just as George Washington had retired to Mount Vernon, Lafayette moved to Lagrange, where he was pleased at the prospects of living in peace with his family. After five years of prison and two years of exile, he was finally home.

Lafayette's tranquillity was disrupted on December 14, 1799, by the death of George Washington, his war companion and mentor. Added to his shock at the loss was hurt — for Napoleon Bonaparte did not invite him to the French memorial service.

In spite of such pettiness, the first consul, feeling more secure in his position, wanted to appoint Lafayette to a senate seat. Lafayette politely refused but did not discourage others from accepting such an offer. At a future date, he also declined the ambassadorship to the United States because of conflicting loyalties. Nevertheless, Bonaparte and Lafayette liked each other personally and often met at social functions; sometimes they talked for hours about politics. Bonaparte was the pragmatic analyst; Lafayette, the staunch defender of freedom. During a reception at the home of Joseph Bonaparte, Lafayette told the first consul that the French people were more than ready for liberty, adding, "It is up to you to give it; it is from you that we await it."

To show Napoleon Bonaparte that he meant to retire from public life, Lafayette resigned his army commission (receiving a 6,000-livres — $30,000 — pension) and devoted most of his time to his own affairs. He continued to speak out on questions of principle, however, and in the 1802 plebiscite, or proposal vote, voted against a consulship for life for

Bonaparte. In the voters' register he added this explanation: "I cannot vote for such an office until civil liberties are guaranteed. Then I will vote for Napoleon Bonaparte." (The results, however, were overwhelmingly in favor: 3,568,000 for, 9,000 against.)

After the United States purchased the Louisiana Territory from France, in 1803, President Jefferson offered his old friend Lafayette the governorship of Louisiana as well as a generous land grant. Lafayette regretfully declined for family and health reasons and chiefly because he "could not shirk his duty to French liberty." He settled his various real estate claims with the French government, including selling the state his land in Guyana, South America, under the condition that the black field hands would remain free. He also enthusiastically supervised the farm, planting rye, tobacco, and wheat; raising pigs and cattle; and experimenting with new hybrids. The enterprises quickly became highly successful.

Family life, too, gave him great pleasure. In 1802, his son, George, married Emilie de Tracy, the daughter of a liberal political philosopher and academician. Anastasie had another daughter, and Virginie, now a young woman of 20, met and fell in love with a young soldier, Louis de Lasteyrie, "a handsome young man, kind, brave, and well educated," wrote Adrienne's sister, Pauline de Montagu. The wedding took place in the spring of 1803; that same season, Lafayette's daughter-in-law, Emilie, gave birth to a little girl. And Diane de Simiane, with whom Lafayette had begun a relationship 20 years before that was to last another two decades, came to visit so often that his children called her "Aunt."

Whenever visitors dropped in to discuss the regime of the recently crowned emperor Napoleon, Lafayette would respond noncommittally. Yet his refusal to discuss the situation spoke volumes.

Sadly, the peaceful, loving environment of Lagrange could not protect Adrienne from the ravages of her prison years. She fell gravely ill, and despite valiant efforts by the emperor's personal physician, she died on Christmas Eve 1807, at the age of 48.

During Napoleon's rule, Lafayette remained largely aloof from politics. He stayed for the most part at his home at Lagrange, a 14th-century castle complete with turrets and a moat, located some 30 miles east of Paris.

Her "six short years of happiness" had come to an end. Devastated, Lafayette closed off her room and was the only one allowed to enter it on various anniversary dates, when he meditated there.

In Adrienne, Lafayette had lost much more than a wife and helpmate. She had been his most ardent adviser and defender, sacrificing her own happiness for his; forgiving, even tolerating his unfaithfulness; selflessly jeopardizing her health and her life to sustain him. "You are not a Christian?" Adrienne asked him one day. "Oh! I know what you are: you're a Fayettist." When he responded that she, too, was one, she replied: "Oh, yes! With all my soul. I feel I could give my life for this sect!"

Under his wife's gentle influence, Lafayette had refrained from criticizing Napoleon, but now he became freer and more outspoken. Nevertheless, he was still completely removed from politics and continued to devote his time to running the farm and the château, surrounded by his family, who lived nearby.

U.S. president Thomas Jefferson offered Lafayette the governorship of Louisiana and a generous land grant after the United States purchased the territory from France in 1803. Lafayette declined, but Jefferson later persuaded him to take the land to pay his mounting debts.

At this time Napoleon was in the process of conquering all of Europe and indeed seemed invincible — until he met with both a cunning Russian army and the fierce Russian winter. Retreating quickly, the emperor was next defeated by yet another coalition in the Battle of Leipzig (October 16–19, 1813). He was forced to abdicate in April 1814 and go into exile on the island of Elba, off the Italian coast. Louis XVIII, brother of the guillotined Louis XVI, ascended to the throne.

Lafayette was more than willing to support a monarchy provided it endorsed a constitution and a bill of rights. The new king, however, refused to grant freedom of the press or to wear the symbolic tricolor cockade. Moreover, he was bent on turning the clock back by reinstituting the privileges of the aristoc-

Louis XVIII, brother of Louis XVI, ascended to the throne after Napoleon's abdication on April 6, 1814. The king was forced to uphold a constitutional monarchy, with a two-house legislature, religious toleration, and constitutional rights for all citizens.

racy abolished during the Revolution 25 years before. The royal Bourbon family, to Lafayette's amazement, had learned nothing.

While Louis XVIII was working to consolidate his regime, Napoleon escaped from Elba and rushed to Paris to reclaim his crown. All along the route he was cheered and congratulated as a liberator. As the emperor entered Paris on March 20, 1815, the royal family wisely fled to Belgium. Lafayette, who was in the capital in case he was needed, according to one account "stayed three days so he would not appear to be afraid and then retired again to Lagrange."

Napoleon grudgingly accepted the concept of elections, and both Lafayette and his son were sent to the Chamber of Representatives, where the former

After his brief return to power, Napoleon was defeated by the British army at the Battle of Waterloo on June 18, 1815. He was exiled to the remote island of Saint Helena in the South Atlantic, where he died in 1821.

was elected its vice-president. The allied forces of Russia, Prussia, Austria, and Britain, embroiled in battle against the French, were determined to bring Napoleon down. On June 18 allied armies, under the leadership of the Duke of Wellington, defeated Napoleon in the Battle of Waterloo (in Belgium), which marked the end of the Napoleonic Wars.

Throwing himself into the fray, in an impassioned speech to his National Assembly colleagues Lafayette demanded the emperor's immediate abdication and even threatened to have him dethroned if he refused to step down voluntarily. Defeated at Waterloo, defeated in Parlement, Napoleon sadly left for a final exile, on the British island of St. Helena, in the south Atlantic, on June 22, 1815. His final 100 days of imperial rule were over.

7

Rebel with a Cause

In the wake of the allied victory at Waterloo and of Napoleon's fall and subsequent exile, the Bourbons returned on July 8, 1815, from their Belgian refuge. Lafayette tried desperately to force the king's hand by having him endorse the Declaration of the Rights of Man and Citizen but found the doors of the Chamber of Deputies locked and guarded. He vainly protested such highhanded conduct and, as soon as he could, left in disgust for Lagrange and another retirement.

King Louis XVIII, though reactionary, was intelligent. He had seen how quickly the French had rallied to Napoleon a year before and consequently was now prepared to accept a more liberal Charter than he had at his first restoration. More important still, he wanted to reconcile the experiences of the Revolution and the empire with a return to a limited monarchical rule, in spite of the increasingly strident objections of his brother, the Count of Artois (the future Charles X) and the far-right deputies, or ultraroyalists, who demanded a pre-1789-style absolutism.

> *My duty orders me to respond to the public trust and to devote myself to the common cause.*
> —MARQUIS DE LAFAYETTE

After the fall of Napoleon, Lafayette returned to political life in full force. He was elected to the Chamber of Deputies and became an outspoken advocate of liberal reform.

Crowds rush to greet Louis XVIII as he returned to assume the throne on July 8, 1815. Wearied by Napoleon's wars, the public welcomed the return of the monarchy and some much-needed stability for France.

At Lagrange, Lafayette was seething with pent-up anger at every slight committed against liberty. At the first opportunity he ran for the Chamber of Deputies and was elected in 1818, much to the king's displeasure. Lafayette sat with like-minded colleagues, always speaking out for the right of citizens — including women — to vote and for total freedom of the press. To his stand against slavery he added a demand for prison reforms and the abolition of the death penalty.

The early 1820s were a period of attempted *coups d'état* (violent overthrows of existing governments), revolutions, and insurrections. Lafayette's name was often connected to these plots, and the secret police did their best to uncover ties that would once and for all silence this unyielding enemy of the regime. However, no criminal evidence was found.

Lafayette was a leading member of the ruling body of the French Carbonari, a secret society modeled after its Italian revolutionary counterpart. He not only gave money to the cause but was instrumental in organizing a Bourbon overthrow. Scheduled for December 29, 1821, three attacks were planned, one at the Fortress of Vincennes in Paris, another at Saumur and Nantes in western France, and a third at Belfort, in the east. After meditating in Adrienne's room on the anniversary of her death, Lafayette left for Belfort, where a provisional government was to be declared, with him at its head.

Unfortunately, a few days before, gunpowder had exploded at Vincennes, thus bringing military reinforcements to the fortress. At Saumur, too, few men took part in the action, and they were quickly rounded up and jailed; at Belfort, a suspicious commander discovered the operation and arrested the officers and soldiers involved.

En route to Belfort, Lafayette was informed about the fiasco. He destroyed all incriminating documents on his person and rode on, ostensibly to visit an old friend. His abandoned carriage had been recognized and impounded by the police, but confederates were able to break into the yard and burn it. This scare did not restrain the champion of democracy, however — he would continue to help anyone who wanted to reestablish liberty in the land.   After he presented himself for reelection, Lafayette was returned to his seat in 1822. Without success, he spoke against undeserved pensions and

Colonel Caron was arrested by the National Guard in 1822 after being implicated in a plot to murder the royal family. During the early 1800s there were numerous attempts by disgruntled republicans — including Lafayette himself — to overthrow the government.

The four sergeants of La Rochelle were executed on September 21, 1822, after they attempted to instigate a military rebellion. Lafayette and a few of his deputies were implicated in the plot but they escaped trial.

privileges, the irresponsible budget, and helping the Spanish king Ferdinand VII in his military restoration of absolute monarchy. After an easy victory in Spain, Louis XVIII felt confident enough to dissolve the Chamber of Deputies and call for new elections in 1824. A wave of conservatism was evident throughout France as electors (only wealthy taxpayers were enfranchised to vote) became more interested in maintaining the status quo. Running on his record and the same liberal platform, Lafayette was defeated by the government candidate. He would now devote most of his time to running his farm, playing with his grandchildren, and writing to his correspondents all over the world.

One such correspondent was U.S. president James Monroe. In the name of the U.S. Congress and the American people, Monroe invited Lafayette to come celebrate 50 years of independence. The marquis and his son sailed on July 13, 1824, to the happy noise of cheering crowds, and arrived in America a month later. If Lafayette's last visit in 1784 had been a triumph, this journey was to be a combination of hero worship and deification from the moment he set foot in New York Harbor to the day, some 13 months later, he returned to France.

In the 50 years since the Battle of Bunker Hill, the United States had prospered and become a vast country of 24 states and more than 10 million people. No upheaval had torn the political and social fabric and brought about terror and death, as had happened in France.

Lafayette, with his larger-than-life presence, not only symbolized for the American people a glorious past of sacrifice and determination but also embodied the very principles on which the republic had been founded. Everywhere Major General Lafayette went (and he tirelessly toured all 24 states), the crowds went wild with enthusiasm and affection. Old veterans of Valley Forge and Yorktown and little children alike came by the thousands to pay their grateful respects to the war hero, the martyr of despotism, the champion of liberty and democracy.

With his hand on the globe, U.S. president James Monroe argues that the United States should not interfere in European affairs.

During his visit to the United States in 1824, Lafayette visited George Washington's tomb at Mount Vernon. There he reflected on how much Washington had achieved and how far France still had to go in becoming a liberated republic.

In addition to countless banquets, balls, fireworks, gun salutes, parades, speeches (that he both made and heard), gifts, and banners, Lafayette was honored by having counties, towns, and streets named after him. He had long and pleasant stays with two former presidents (Jefferson and Madison) and two future chief executives (Jackson and Van Buren — Jackson called the meeting "the greatest moment of my life"). He went alone to George Washington's grave site at Mount Vernon, returning with his eyes filled with tears. He was also the first in a line of distinguished foreigners to address a joint session of Congress.

Past and present presidents also showed their high regard for Lafayette. The outgoing chief executive, James Monroe, was instrumental in having Congress almost unanimously award the marquis a cash grant of $200,000 ($2.5 million in 1987 dollars) and a land grant of 24,000 acres. Both gifts were much appreciated: Lafayette's financial situation was precarious, because he had been spending freely in support of liberal causes all over Europe and Latin America, mortgaging Lagrange, his farm, and holdings in Brittany. As a supreme tribute, Jefferson, Monroe, and the newly elected president, John Quincy Adams, gathered in the rebuilt White House to celebrate Lafayette's 68th birthday. Then, on September 8, 1825, after tearful farewells, Lafayette and his son boarded a navy frigate, christened the *Brandywine*, said Lafayette, "to recall my first battle."

When the ship landed in France on October 3 to another roaring welcome, not only did Lafayette seem rejuvenated, but his reputation was on the rise again. Louis XVIII had died in 1824, and Charles X (the former Count of Artois) was now on the throne. Of mediocre intelligence and autocratic views, the new king tried to reestablish to the greatest extent feasible an absolute monarchy — from an outmoded coronation at Rheims to increased police powers to restored privileges and titles of nobility.

To a man just returned from the land of liberty, the royal government seemed authoritarian and reactionary, and Lafayette became the unofficial spokesman of liberation movements everywhere. Had he not made, on the 50th anniversary of the Battle of Bunker Hill, a widely publicized toast "to the liberation of Europe"? Italians, Poles, Greeks, Portuguese, Germans, Spaniards — all came to Lagrange to receive his moral and financial support. He wrote long letters to Simon Bolívar, the "*Libertador*" of South America, to encourage him in his patriotic pursuits.

Elected in June 1827 to his old seat in the Chamber, Lafayette seized the occasion of an opposition leader's funeral, attended by more than 100,000 mourners, to prove to the regime that the dedication

Lafayette aided the South American liberator Simon Bolívar in his effort to free the Spanish colonies. Until his death, Lafayette remained an ardent supporter of liberal causes throughout Europe and Latin America.

After the death of Louis XVIII, his brother Charles X took the throne. Having spent the revolutionary years in exile, Charles returned to France embittered and ready to restore the divine authority of the king and Catholic church.

and passion of this 70-year-old fighter had not waned in the least: "It is by the tomb of this faithful servant of the people that we must show our respect and commitment to man's inalienable rights."

Charles X was becoming more and more unpopular, and he and his family were often jeered in public. Unable to get his programs approved by the deputies in the Chamber, the king called for new elections and was faced with an even greater opposition in the new body. He therefore chose a new prime minister, one somewhat more moderate in outlook. Yet the main demands for wider suffrage, freedom of the press, and mandatory education remained unmet, much to the liberals' angry disappointment. Displeased with the present state of affairs and badly advised, Charles X believed he could rule by decree. He dismissed his cabinet and named Prince Jules de Polignac as his prime minister in August 1829, while setting new elections for January 23, 1830.

Lafayette was on a triumphant tour of central and southeastern France when he heard about the new ministerial appointment. He immediately understood that the king meant to tear up the constitutional Charter granted by Louis XVIII and to restore a pre-1789 absolute monarchy. In a much-applauded speech in Lyons, Lafayette reminded his audience and King Charles that "the French nation knows its rights and will know how to defend them."

The new elections only increased the number of liberal deputies, but the adamant king refused any compromise with the opposition and instead dissolved the Chamber and again called for new elections. He and Polignac hoped to buy enough votes through pensions and patronage to reclaim their right-wing majority. They also hoped that the conquest of Algeria, then under way, would distract public opinion from their repeated violations of the Charter.

As district after district returned the same liberal representatives (including Lafayette), the government decided to wait for a propitious moment to strike. The capture of Algiers by the French army on July 5, 1830, provided just such an opportunity. On July 25, Charles X issued four decrees, suspending freedom of the press, dissolving the newly elected (but unconvened) Chamber, severely limiting electoral franchise, reducing the number of deputies, and setting the date of elections for September.

As soon as the four ordinances were published, workers and students gathered in the streets of Paris, occasionally throwing cobblestones at soldiers and police and erecting barricades. In response, the troops shot back, killing or wounding several rebels. The revolution had begun. Lafayette, for his part, rushed back from Lagrange to Paris and arrived on the evening of July 27. After he was elected commander of the National Guard, he toured the barricades and held numerous discussions with legislative colleagues. Some were willing to give the king another chance, provided he would rescind his decrees. Others decided he had put himself in an illegal position and therefore was no longer to be obeyed.

On July 5, 1830, the French army captured the city of Algiers in North Africa. Charles and his prime minister, Prince Jules de Polignac, used the military success to divert domestic opposition from the king's growing authoritarianism.

The situation was changing very rapidly, as the popular forces, often with horrendous losses, seized most military positions all over Paris during the *Trois Glorieuses*, the three glorious days of the revolution. Behind-the-scenes negotiations were taking place between Charles X and royalist factions, who advised granting a bill of rights. In fact, it was too late for the king. Lafayette had already declared, "The royal family has ceased to reign." Liberal deputies, on the other hand, preferred a true constitutional monarchy along English lines and were seeking to convince Louis-Philippe, Duke of Orléans, to accept the throne. There was also Lafayette, who, but for the asking, could easily become president of an American-type republic. Partly because he was not a "governor," partly because he judged France not ready for the American experiment (an opinion shared by the U.S. ambassador himself), he hardly considered the possibility.

During the three days known as Les Trois Glorieuses (July 27–29, 1830) workers and students set up barricades in the streets to protest the king's July Ordinances. Soon soldiers joined them, and the popular revolt became a full-blown insurrection.

On July 31, 1830, promising to uphold the Charter, the Duke of Orléans, dressed in his lieutenant general's uniform, a tricolor cockade on his hat, rode to City Hall to meet with Lafayette. The crowd wanted a republic and was therefore hostile to any monarchical compromise. Only Lafayette's endorsement of Louis-Philippe could prevent anarchy, perhaps civil war, and possible involvement of the European powers. So, much as he had saved Louis XVI and Marie Antoinette by presenting them to the mob on October 6, 1789, Lafayette wrapped a tricolor flag around the duke, led him to the balcony, and there embraced him to the shouts of "Long live the Duke of Orléans! Long live Lafayette!"

"We have made a beautiful and quick revolution," Lafayette wrote a friend. "All its glory belongs to the people of Paris." Yes, the revolution was over. Louis-Philippe was going to govern according to principles Lafayette had been advocating for some 50 years. The dawn of a new age, filled with hope, was breaking.

Louis-Philippe, on horseback, waves to unruly crowds at the Palais Royal, Paris, on his way to Versailles, where he was proclaimed King of the French. Although the people wanted a republic, Lafayette endorsed Louis-Philippe, believing that a constitutional monarchy would provide greater stability.

8

A Liberal Betrayed

Louis-Philippe was the son of the Duke of Orléans, whose title he later inherited. His father, of
the younger branch of the Bourbons, was full of
revolutionary zeal but was sent to the guillotine by
Robespierre and his Jacobin colleagues, who feared
that the man who sat in the National Assembly with
the Third Estate actually wanted to rule France.

The son, too, had rallied to democratic principles.
Under General Charles-François Dumouriez, he had
fought valiantly at Valmy and Jemappes. Implicated
in his commander's betrayal, however, he had to
flee abroad in 1793. He lived in Switzerland, Scan-
dinavia, the United States, England, and Sicily, returning to France in 1815. Never a part of the
Restoration governments of Louis XVIII and Charles
X, the Duke of Orléans associated with liberal deputies, businessmen, and newspaper publishers.

> *Liberty, equality and public
> order has always been
> my motto.*
> —MARQUIS DE LAFAYETTE

**Lafayette posed for a portrait in his later years at his
country estate, Lagrange. Increasingly disaffected with
the king, Lafayette resumed his retirement and kept up
his voluminous correspondence with liberal supporters
around the world.**

Prime Minister Jules de Polignac's efforts to reestablish papal and royal authority in France led to his imprisonment in 1830 during the July Revolution and his eventual exile in 1845.

Very cleverly, he had presented himself as the heir of the ideals of 1789. A born politician, he believed that form appealed to people more than substance. For example, rather than ride in his carriage, he would walk, often in the company of his wife and children, like any other middle-class family; like his common-man counterpart, he would dress in everyday clothes and carry an umbrella.

In 1830, because Charles X was no longer able to govern and Lafayette was unwilling to assume presidential leadership, a well-orchestrated campaign — financed by the Duke of Orléans — to have himself named lieutenant general and regent was organized. With riots exploding all over Paris, liberal deputies and businessmen begged the duke to take power and save France from chaos and war.

The cunning Louis-Philippe had realized that support from such law-and-order quarters was not enough to overcome popular resentment toward any member of the royal family, however distant. Only Lafayette's endorsement could guarantee early approval of a Bourbon from the masses. To this end he promised anything Lafayette wanted to hear ("the Charter will henceforth be a reality"), and the old general listened with pleasure to all the right phrases.

With embraces and flag wrapping, Lafayette had conferred on Louis-Phillipe the full legitimacy of his form of liberalism. After all, during a conversation they held that very same evening (July 31, 1830), both agreed that what was needed was "a popular throne, surrounded with thoroughly republican institutions." Lafayette was thus convinced of the duke's sincerity. Soon a system adapted from the American model would be established, he foresaw, one which would include a more broadly elected Assembly, an elected (not appointed) Senate, ministerial responsibility, freedom of the press and of religion, and reorganization of the National Guard.

Once Charles X had left France for his English exile, the Duke of Orléans ascended the throne as Louis-Philippe I, King of the French (rather than King of France) in a simple civil ceremony, surrounded by tricolor flags and attended by representatives from the two chambers. After a brief speech,

Victor Hugo was among the many intellectuals who maintained a correspondence with Lafayette. One of the most important French Romantic writers, Hugo was also a lifelong supporter of republican ideals.

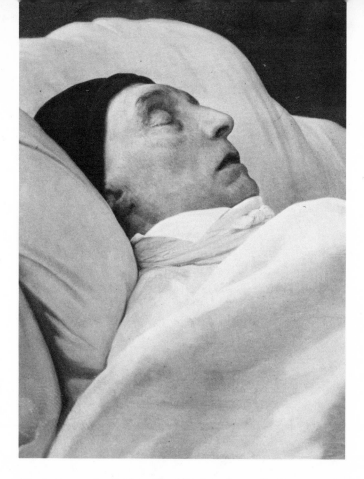

Lafayette contracted pneumonia after attending the funeral of a friend in early 1834. He died on May 20 at the age of 77, after spending nearly 60 years of his life promoting the cause of liberty.

the "citizen-king," as he liked to be called, swore to uphold the new Charter. Lafayette could not have been more pleased: "Here is the king we needed. Here is the most republican leader we could have had."

Although Lafayette had just been confirmed in his rank as commandant-general of the National Guard and was at the height of his popularity, he was slowly being undermined by fellow deputies, who wanted to maintain law and order at all costs, and by the king himself. Louis-Philippe wanted to consolidate his rule but was afraid to move too fast and risk a confrontation with Lafayette. Legislators and king got their chance when Lafayette mishandled the protective custody of Charles X's jailed ministers.

Polignac and his cabinet had been arrested after the "three glorious days" of July to stand trial, and despite warnings and threats of mob violence Lafayette did little to ensure their safety. Other National Guard officers, however, were able to avert tragedy by spiriting the ministers away to a more secure prison. Rather than dismiss the National Guard's commandant-general outright, which might have caused a riot, the deputies abolished the post altogether. Lafayette was hurt by this maneuver, so obviously aimed at him, and resigned on December 25, 1830, in the hope that the people would beg him to reconsider, as they had done in 1789 and again in 1791. This time, however, his tactic did not succeed, and a very relieved Louis-Philippe accepted the resignation with "much regret."

Nevertheless, because he had been elected to the Chamber, Lafayette could continue to lobby for the causes close to his heart. For example, he spoke out against the death penalty and the slave trade ("a crime against God and humanity"); he wanted to free the oppressed of the world and worked hard, but in vain, on behalf of Italian and Polish inde-

A satirical lithograph by Honoré Daumier caricatures Louis-Philippe outwardly weeping at Lafayette's funeral while exclaiming under his breath, "Ha! You're done for, old fellow." The "citizen king" was more than happy to be rid of Lafayette, whom he considered an irritating symbol of liberty and republican ideals.

pendence; and always he made speeches about liberty and the need for constant vigilance to preserve it, lest it be destroyed by despots.

Hostility from the king, who denied he ever agreed to "thoroughly republican institutions," and indifference from his colleagues and the middle class, who sought to put the regime's new motto ("Get rich!") into practice, disillusioned Lafayette greatly. Although he still used every opportunity to lash out at Louis-Philippe, even declaring that "the king broke his word to me, and through me to the people," Lafayette was, for all intents and purposes, fully retired.

Louis-Philippe and his wife, Maria Amelia, leave Paris after his abdication on February 24, 1848. He was forced off the throne by a revolt of the lower and middle classes after he refused to grant them the right to vote.

Now in his mid-70s, he lived mostly on his estate, where he began writing his memoirs (more than 3,000 printed pages). He also maintained a voluminous correspondence with the leaders and intellectuals of his time (Presidents Adams and Jackson, Lord Palmerston, Count Ostrowski, Giuseppe Mazzini, Washington Irving, and Victor Hugo, among others). He enjoyed visitors (James Fenimore Cooper had his own room at Lagrange) and family gatherings — with his 3 children and their spouses, 11 grandchildren, and 12 great-grandchildren. It was not uncommon at Lagrange, therefore, for him to see 25 people for dinner several times a week.

Commandant-General Lafayette stands before the troops of the National Guard. Few world leaders enjoyed as much fame abroad or as much popularity at home as Lafayette, a dedicated champion of freedom.

On February 1, 1834, Lafayette attended funeral services for a friend and colleague, and harsh winter wind or not, he insisted on following the procession on foot. He caught a bad cold, which worsened into pneumonia. Four months later, feeling recovered enough to go for a ride, he again caught cold. Despite constant care, he could not recover. With his hand tight around Adrienne's miniature portrait, Lafayette died on May 20, 1834. He was almost 77 years old.

The funeral cortege included dignitaries from all branches of the government and from the army. Crowds lined up all along the procession route. Three thousand National Guardsmen followed the bier, which was carried by Polish refugees and accompanied by relatives and a U.S. delegation. Lafayette was buried in the Picpus cemetery next to his wife, and American earth he had brought back in 1825 was sprinkled on top of the coffin.

Even if the official French conduct was quite dignified, the opposition press accused the king of being more than happy to be finally rid of this irritating symbol of liberty and republican ideals. For instance, Honoré Daumier, the famous lithographer, published a print in which a smirking Louis-Philippe sheds crocodile tears while thinking, "Ha! You're done for, old fellow." On the other hand, the United States ordered that all flags be flown at half-mast and a 30-day period of mourning observed. Former president John Quincy Adams received the painful honor of delivering the eulogy to a joint session of Congress. Since 1834, on every May 20th the American ambassador to France has paid loyal homage to the great patriot's memory at a simple graveside ceremony.

At the end of 1830, a few months after Louis-Philippe had come to power thanks to his hypocritical adoption of the Revolution's ideals, Lafayette had warned him that the people would not wait much longer for true democracy. Indeed, fewer than 20 years later, in February 1848, Lafayette's prophecy came true: The citizen-king was swept away by another popular uprising in the February Revolution. The Bourbon Dynasty had come to an end.

Further Reading

Beahrs, Virginia Oakley. *The Fire and the Glory*. Philadelphia: Westminster, 1976.

Bruns, Roger. *George Washington*. New York: Chelsea House, 1987.

Carson, S. L. *Maximilien Robespierre*. New York: Chelsea House, 1988.

Dwyer, Frank. *Georges Jacques Danton*. New York: Chelsea House, 1987.

Gerson, Noel B. *Statue in Search of a Pedestal*. New York: Dodd Mead, 1976.

Gottschalk, Louis R. *Lafayette and the Close of the American Revolution*. Chicago: University of Chicago Press, 1965.

———. *Lafayette Between the American and the French Revolution*. Chicago: University of Chicago Press, 1965.

———. *Lafayette Comes to America*. Chicago: University of Chicago Press, 1965.

———. *Lafayette Joins the American Army*. Chicago: University of Chicago Press, 1965.

———, and Margaret Maddox. *Lafayette in the French Revolution*. 2 vols. Chicago: University of Chicago Press, 1969 and 1973.

Holbrook, Sabra. *Lafayette, Man in the Middle*. New York: Atheneum, 1977.

Idzerda, Stanley J., ed. *Lafayette in the Age of the American Revolution*. Ithaca, New York: Cornell University Press, 1977.

Klamkin, Marian. *The Return of Lafayette: 1824–1825*. New York: Scribners, 1975.

La Fuye, Maurice de. *The Apostle of Liberty*. New York: T. Yoseloff, 1956.

Latzko, Andreas. *Lafayette*. Garden City, New York: Doubleday, 1936.

Loveland, Anne C. *Emblem of Liberty*. Baton Rouge: Louisiana State University Press, 1971.

Maurios, André. *Adrienne: The Life of the Marquise de La Fayette*. New York: McGraw-Hill, 1961.

Thompson, J. M. *The French Revolution*. London: Oxford University Press, 1943.

Chronology

Sept. 6, 1757	Lafayette born at Castle of Chavaniac
1770	Inherits vast fortune from grandfather
April 11, 1774	Marries Adrienne d'Ayen-Noailles
June 13, 1777	Sails to Charleston, South Carolina, to help fight in revolutionary war
Aug. 1, 1777	Meets George Washington
Sept. 11, 1777	Distinguishes himself at Battle of Brandywine
Feb. 6, 1779	Returns to France
April 28, 1780	Comes back to America with arms and troops
Oct. 19, 1781	Helps Washington defeat Cornwallis at Yorktown
Dec. 23, 1781	Departs from United States after being declared "Hero of Two Worlds"
Sept. 3, 1783	United States and England declare peace, signing Treaty of Paris
Aug. 4–Dec. 21, 1784	Lafayette visits United States
July 11, 1789	Presents *Declaration of the Rights of Man and Citizen*
July 14, 1789	Mob storms Bastille prison, starting French Revolution
	Lafayette elected commandant-general of National Guard
Aug. 1792	Robespierre orders Lafayette arrested
	Lafayette seeks refuge and is arrested by the Austrians
Oct. 15, 1795	Adrienne and daughters join Lafayette at Olmütz fortress
Sept. 19, 1796	Lafayette freed from prison
1799	Returns to France
May 10, 1814	Elected to Chamber of Deputies
June 1815	Helps force Napoleon Bonaparte into exile
1818	Reelected to Chamber of Deputies
Aug. 14, 1824–Sept. 8, 1825	Visits United States for the last time
July 25, 1830	Charles X signs Four Ordinances, causing a revolution
	Lafayette elected commandant-general of National Guard
July 31, 1830	Anoints Duke of Orléans King Louis-Philippe
Dec. 24, 1830	Lafayette resigns
May 20, 1834	Lafayette dies in Paris

Index

Arthur M. Schlesinger, jr., taught history at Harvard for many years and is currently Albert Schweitzer Professor of the Humanities at City University of New York. He is the author of numerous highly praised works in American history and has twice been awarded the Pulitzer Prize. He served in the White House as special assistant to Presidents Kennedy and Johnson.

Pierre L. Horn was born in Paris, France, where he studied at the Lycée Voltaire. He received his M.A. and Ph.D. from Columbia University and is currently on the faculty at Wright State University, Ohio. Named a *Chevalier dans l'Ordre des Palmes Académiques* by the French government in 1978, Professor Horn has written extensively on French literature and culture. He is the author of *Louis XIV* in the Chelsea House series WORLD LEADERS—PAST & PRESENT.

PICTURE CREDITS

Art Resource: pp. 82, 98, 106; Bettmann Archive: pp. 2, 16, 20, 24, 25, 33, 36, 44, 49, 52, 55, 64, 65, 68, 69, 71, 74, 78, 84, 85, 92, 93, 101, 102; Brown Brothers: pp. 23, 26, 30, 86; Bulloz: pp. 34, 50, 53, 57, 60, 61, 76, 95, 97; Cornell University Library: p. 17; Culver Pictures: pp. 32, 38, 39, 58, 62, 63, 70, 72, 91, 96, 100, 104, 105; Giraudon: pp. 46, 48, 56, 75, 88, 94; Historical Pictures Service: pp. 19, 31, 42, 54, 83, 103; Library of Congress: pp. 14, 28, 29; National Graphics Center: p. 81; New-York Historical Society: p. 45; Scala/Art Resource: pp. 15, 21; Snark International: p. 59; Roger Viollet: pp. 12, 18, 22, 66, 89, 90; Virginia Museum: p. 37; Virginia State Library: pp. 40, 41